THE
HEART OF DAVID
JOURNAL

Leading with Vision, Passion, and Wisdom

VOLUME 8

By David Mayorga

Published by

SHABAR PUBLICATIONS
www.shabarpublications.com

Most Shabar Publications products are available at special quantity discounts for bulk purchase for sales promotions, fund-raising and educational needs. For details, write Shabar Publications at mayorga1126@gmail.com.

The Heart of David Journal Volume 8:
Leading with Vision, Passion, and Wisdom
by David Mayorga

Published by Shabar Publications
3833 N. Taylor Rd.
Palmhurst, Texas 78573
www.shabarpublications.com
www.masterbuildertx.com

This book or parts thereof may not be reproduced in any form, stored in a retrieval system, or transmitted in any form by any means - electronic, mechanical, photocopy, recording, or otherwise - without prior written permission of the publisher, except as provided by United States of America copyright law.

Unless otherwise noted, all Scripture quotations are from the New Kings James Version of the Bible. Copyright@1979, 1980, 1982 by Thomas Nelson, Inc., publishers. Used by permission.

Copyright @ 2024 by David Mayorga
All rights reserved

ISBN: 978-1-955433-21-1

Table of Content

Chapter 1: The Cry for Alignment - Part 1! 6

Chapter 2: The Cry for Alignment - Part 2! 11

Chapter 3: The Cry for Alignment - Part 3! 16

Chapter 4: The Cry for Alignment - Part 1! 22

Chapter 5: To Tired to Pray! 27

Chapter 6: Only Believe! 32

Chapter 7: When the Devil Wags His Head at You! 41

Chapter 8: Unlimited Fire! 48

Chapter 9: Learn to Follow the Promise! 54

Chapter 10: Rules to Follow When Pregnant with God! 59

Chapter 11: Impartation of Life! 63

Chapter 12: Where Did the Fire Go? 68

Chapter 13: Fresh Fire! 75

Chapter 14: Get Alone and Wait for Fire! 81

Chapter 15: Who Is In Charge? 85

Chapter 16: It's Getting Late:
              Knowing What Time It Is! 91

Chapter 17: The Time is Now! 95

Chapter 18: Rewired by God! 100

Chapter 19: The Harvest is Ready! 105

Chapter 20: Trained in Character by Obstacles! 112

Chapter 21: Why Is This Happening to Me? 115

Chapter 22: Abide at All Cost! 120

Chapter 23: Stirred! 128

Chapter 24: When Jesus says, "I Don't Know You! . . . 132

Chapter 25: The Passion of God! 139

Chapter 26: More and More! 144

Chapter 27: God's Secret to True Greatness! 148

Chapter 28: Valuable Seeds of the Kingdom! 152

Chapter 29: Nothing is Greater Than God! 157

Chapter 30: Visitations from the Lord! - Part 1 164

Chapter 31: Visitations from the Lord! - Part 2 168

Chapter 32: Visitations from the Lord! - Part 1 173

Chapter 33: A *Burning Bush* Calling! 177

Chapter 34: At the Scent of Water! 182

Chapter 35: God Shares Secrets with
               Those Closes to Him! 186

Chapter 36: Disappointed! 191

Chapter 37: The Right! 195

Chapter 38: Smitten by God! 199

Chapter 39: Time for Renewal! 203

Chapter 40: The Return of An Unclean Spirit
Is a Test of Discipline! 207

Chapter 41: Our Fellowship with Christ
and the Father! - Part 1 211

Chapter 42: Our Fellowship with Christ
and the Father! - Part 1 215

Chapter 43: The Benefit of Strife and Contention! ... 220

Chapter 44: The Calling! 224

Chapter 45: Discerning the Wicked and their Mindset! 228

Chapter 46: Overcoming Earthly Attachments! -
Part 1 232

Chapter 47: Overcoming Earthly Attachments! -
Part 2 237

Chapter 48: Will You Sin Against God?
Character Test 1 241

Chapter 49: Will You Sin Against God?
Character Test 2 245

Chapter 50: The Appreciation of Crumbs! 249

Chapter 51: Learning to Discern
the Burden of Christ ! 254

Chapter 52: Keeping Christ Always at the Center! ... 258

1

The Cry for Alignment! - Part 1

"In the beginning God (prepared, formed, fashioned, and) created the heavens and the earth. The earth was without form and an empty waste, and darkness was upon the face of the very great deep. The Spirit of God was moving (hovering, brooding) over the face of the waters. And God said, let there be light; and there was light. And God saw that the light was good (suitable, pleasant) and He approved it; and God separated the light from the darkness. And God called the light Day, and the darkness He called Night. And there was evening and there was morning, one day." (Genesis 1:1-5 -Amplified Version)

When I think of the word alignment, I think of something that is out of place or out of position; therefore, it must be returned to its proper place. But let us see a bit deeper what the word alignment means.

Oxford's Language dictionary defines alignment as an arrangement in a straight line or correct or appropriate relative positions. It also means part of an agreement or alliance.

Alignment may be a challenging topic of study or meditation, but it has everything to do with your life today. Enough to say that if you and I are out of alignment, we will struggle in countless ways.

We must learn what alignment means and how it affects our personal and professional lives. You will discover how impacting it can be if we align our lives with God's will or how damning and destructive the consequences will be without it!

Where Does Alignment Begin?

I'm not a scientist, and I am by no means an authority on the subject matter, but one thing is sure, and this one thing I know: When I am aligned, I know it, and when I am not, I also know it! Can you perceive this in your own life?

Since I am not a scientist or a specialist on this subject, let me speak to you from the point of view where I believe I can better relate to the topic – from the Holy Scriptures.

Let me take you behind the veil of the metaphysical and into the realm or dimension of the Spirit.

I believe God creates all things. This includes all matters. Our lives, as we know them, our minds, hearts, and very beings, are all made by God and for God. This is God's plan, and it's up to man to discover His God-given destiny in the short and limited time he has here on earth.

The will of God is embedded in your spirit, whether dormant or not. Whether you feel it or not, the desire to spend eternity with God has been deposited in your life.

To agree or disagree based on our religious biases is irrelevant! Ignoring that you were created by God or attributing your being to the theory of evolution is also irrelevant.

You see, as we respond to the promptings of God's Spirit, we are being transformed. Remember, the Holy Spirit is the mind of God. His work is to bring us to the fullness of God as He, the Spirit, coaches us in the ways of God. No one knows what God is thinking, only the Spirit of God. He lives within every born-again believer. He is the One making things align within us.

Most of our struggles can be traced back to a decision, a thought, or an action that didn't align with God's will.

When something is out of line or position, it screams from deep within and sends red lights warning us of an error committed or an assault on God's perfect will for us.

Time after time, we see people hurting, struggling, and acting in specific ways. Why, we ask? The simple and quick answer is alignment. I believe that much of the pain we experience is because we are not aligned with God's will.

When Alignment is Reached!

Why the quest to become aligned and why aligned with God's will? The answer is not too hard to figure out.

Allow me to outline some powerful results or benefits, if you will, of a life that moves in God's alignment:

    1. First, as an aligned individual with God, you can release a more significant or fuller potential of what you are supposed to be.

For example, let us take a marathon runner. If the individual has a dislocated joint and the best thing he can do is walk and not run due to the pain caused by the misalignment, his potential for anything more significant will be questioned.

One can't run if he is barely able to walk.

    2. Secondly, an aligned individual won't have to try hard to fit in or compete with anyone due to their misaligned perception of things. When one is unhealthy, they always feel they must try harder to keep up. When healed, one moves with gratitude and fits in in any situation.

    3. Finally, an aligned individual will be productive. They can move with God and impact whatever they set their heart to do. Have you ever heard the saying that everything they touch turns to gold? These are the results of an aligned individual.

You see, the Lord created us for Himself. We were created with God's intent to be vessels full of His glory. We were placed in this world to reveal His glory. My friends, there is no greater calling that brings joy to the Lord than for us to walk in the fullness of His glory! So, with all within you, work to be aligned with God's will. Neh'enah.

2

The Cry for Alignment – Part 2

"Now there was a certain man of Ramathaim Zophim, of the mountains of Ephraim, and his name was Elkanah the son of Jeroham, the son of Elihu, the son of Tohu, the son of Zuph, an Ephraimite. And he had two wives: the name of one was Hannah, and the name of the other Peninnah. Peninnah had children, but Hannah had no children. This man went up from his city yearly to worship and sacrifice to the LORD of hosts in Shiloh. Also, the two sons of Eli, Hophni and Phinehas, the priests of the LORD, were there. And whenever the time came for Elkanah to make an offering, he would give portions to Peninnah his wife and to all her sons and daughters. But to Hannah he would give a double portion, for he loved Hannah, although the LORD had closed her womb. And her rival also provoked her severely, to make her miserable, because the LORD had closed her womb. So it was, year by year, when she went up to the house of the LORD, that she provoked her; therefore, she wept and did not eat. Then Elkanah her husband said to her, "Hannah, why do you weep? Why do you not eat? And why is your heart grieved? Am I not better to you than ten sons?" So, Hannah arose after they had finished eating and drinking in Shiloh. Now Eli the priest was sitting on the seat by the doorpost of the tabernacle of the

LORD. And she was in bitterness of soul, prayed to the Lord, and wept in anguish. Then she made a vow and said, "O LORD of hosts, if You will indeed look on the affliction of Your maidservant and remember me, and not forget Your maidservant, but will give Your maidservant a male child, then I will give him to the LORD all the days of his life, and no razor shall come upon his head." And it happened, as she continued praying before the LORD, that Eli watched her mouth. Now Hannah spoke in her heart; only her lips moved, but her voice was not heard. Therefore, Eli thought she was drunk. So, Eli said to her, "How long will you be drunk? Put your wine away from you!" But Hannah answered and said, "No, my lord, I am a woman of sorrowful spirit. I have drunk neither wine nor intoxicating drink but have poured out my soul before the LORD. Do not consider your maidservant a wicked woman, for out of the abundance of my complaint and grief I have spoken until now." Then Eli answered and said, "Go in peace, and the God of Israel grant your petition which you have asked of Him." And she said, "Let your maidservant find favor in your sight." So, the woman went her way and ate, and her face was no longer sad." (1 Samuel 1:1-18)

In speaking on alignment, I want to share a bit of what a life without alignment looks like.

The story mentioned above tells us of a situation in the life of a woman named Hannah. This woman was a God-fearing woman who was married to a man named Elkanah.

The Scriptures tell us that Elkanah had two wives, Hannah and Peninnah. It further says that the **"Lord had closed her womb."** In this case, Elkanah was given the right to marry another woman who could have his children; at least, this appears to be the idea. Whether it was allowed or not, Elkanah had two wives. One gave him children, and Hannah did not.

So it came to pass that year after year, her rival, Peninnah, would provoke her, Listen to this: **"And her rival also provoked her severely, to make her miserable, because the LORD had closed her womb. So it was, year by year, when she went up to the house of the LORD, that she provoked her; therefore, she wept and did not eat."**

Anguish!

As if the fact that Hannah's womb had been closed was not bad enough, Peninnah would make fun of her for her difficult situation. These were not happy moments for Hannah and not even for Elkanah. Allow me to go deeper:

As a woman, Hannah wanted children. The reality of being unable to have any did a number on her. As a result of her inability to enter motherhood, she was in anguish. She was shredded to pieces by this fact.

Elkanah describes this anguish, this brokenness, if you look at it.

How Not Being Aligned Looks Like!

Then Elkanah her husband said to her, **"Hannah, why do you weep? Why do you not eat? And why is your heart grieved? Am I not better to you than ten sons?"**

As we walk in our journey with God, we will face many tests and challenges and be at our wits end more than we know.

In the case of Hannah, she knew she was created to be so much more and have so much more than what she did. She knew that motherhood was her portion and that motherhood was supposed to happen to her!

Everything wrong inside of us will manifest itself eventually. Hannah was not buying the idea that her womb was closed. She knew something was out of alignment! No wonder she was in anguish of soul; she was out of sync.

Elkanah saw his wife hurting. Her anguish and pain would increase yearly until she sought God for clarity.

Elkanah saw this in his wife: sadness, continual weeping, no appetite, and a grieved heart. Nothing on this earth would appease her broken and anguished heart. Something was off, out of line, and she would figure it out somehow.

Alignment Brings Joy!

When we align with what we sense, joy will fill our hearts—an indescribable joy full of glory!

As Hannah spent time in God's presence, her heart found alignment with God and started finding answers to her sadness, weeping, and grieving heart. As she continued to pour her anguish before the Lord, the Lord came through with a glorious breakthrough.

It won't be easy to experience real peace and joy until you know you have entered alignment.

Many are content to live out of sync with God's will, others are happy to live out of alignment with their life assignment, and others have just surrendered in the fight to take what is theirs and settled for second best.

My friend, we don't have to live out of alignment or continue living short of God's best. Neh'enah.

3

The Cry for Alignment! – Part 3

"Now they came to Jericho. As He went out of Jericho with His disciples and a great multitude, blind Bartimaeus, the son of Timaeus, sat by the road begging. And when he heard that it was Jesus of Nazareth, he began to cry out and say, "Jesus, Son of David, have mercy on me!" Then, many warned him to be quiet, but he cried out all the more, "Son of David, have mercy on me!" So, Jesus stood still and commanded him to be called. Then they called the blind man, saying to him, "Be of good cheer. Rise. He is calling you." And throwing aside his garment, he rose and came to Jesus. So Jesus answered and said to him, "What do you want Me to do for you?" The blind man said to Him, "Rabboni, that I may receive my sight." Then Jesus said to him, "Go your way; your faith has made you well." And immediately he received his sight and followed Jesus on the road." (Mark 10:46-52)

While meditating on the theme of alignment, the Holy Spirit brought to my attention another man who longed for alignment. I am speaking to you of Bartimaeus; this man was blind!

What about Bartimaeus? How is this man's life relevant to

the subject of alignment?

Let me show you what I believe the Holy Spirit is saying to us on this subject and how Bartimaeus is a type of believer who lives today out of alignment with God's intended initially.

A Man Who Sat by the Road

Bartimaeus' life was pretty much set, and to be brutally honest, there was nothing more to do but sit by the side of the road and beg. Beg for money and food, perhaps, but this was done daily. Was this normal for a blind man to do? Was it just another poor man in the crowd of thousands? For Bartimaeus to sit by the side of the road, begging had become the norm, and for people to pass by his way was also typical.

It is easy to get accustomed to living a life of pain, struggle, and suffering. Most people who suffer in any way today get used to life that way. They think to themselves that nothing will ever change. Living this kind of life is easy when no one provokes us. We can stay in our condition until the kingdom comes!

Sometimes, people come along the way and stir us out of our comfort zone, and we don't appreciate it. We get upset and try to explain and excuse our condition so we can stay as we are! In the case of blind Bartimaeus, he was not making excuses – he was blind and didn't want to remain in that condition any longer.

He Cried All the More!

"And when he heard that it was Jesus of Nazareth, he began to cry out and say, "Jesus, Son of David, have mercy on me!" Then many warned him to be quiet, but he cried out all the more...."

Let me say here: A reaction is provoked when Jesus is in the vicinity! When the presence of God comes, everything around submits, and things that are not aligned or out of place begin to make their way to their rightful place.

This is what I believe happened to this blind man.

The Scripture says that when **"he heard that it was Jesus of Nazareth, he began to cry out and say…"**. What caused the reaction or the provocation? What stirred this man's heart to cry out and say, **"Jesus, Son of David, have mercy on me?"**

A Cry Was Made!

As Jesus passed by, this man's deep cry came out. Something in him needed to come forth –the cry for alignment and God's divine order. The time to continue living blind had finally ended, and his spirit knew it. He cried out, it says.

What does cry out mean?

In its original Greek, the words cry out means to croak. To croak means to make a rough or raucous sound. It is based on the croaking of ravens. To groan deeply. To be dissatisfied. It is used in childbirth. It is a war cry, as when Joshua captured Jericho.

Interestingly, the people around him, including the disciples with Jesus, didn't recognize the war cry, the deep groans of the spirit! This is typical of most believers today. They are clueless when understanding the groanings of the Spirit of God. Listen to this: **"Then many warned him to be quiet, but he cried out all the more...."**

What are those to do who don't understand the groanings of God? They do what they do best – they try to shut it up! They told Bartimaeus to be quiet. Without their knowledge, they were quieting the deep cry of childbirth in this man!

I think the enemy is the only one interested in keeping you quiet. He doesn't want you to touch God's presence; the devil knows what God's presence provokes very well!

Time to Arise!

"So Jesus stood still and commanded him to be called. Then they called the blind man, saying to him, "Be of good cheer. Rise. He is calling you." And throwing aside his garment, he rose and came to Jesus."

Nothing gets the attention of God quicker than when His servants are crying out for alignment to do His will. Once you know what to do with God's revelation, Jesus wants to empower you. Once you realize that you need alignment and are not content with how things have been, watch out; God will move powerfully in you.

As Jesus called Bartimaeus, he threw aside his garment and rose. I believe there comes a time when we must throw aside the garment, that ugly cloak of flesh and self, and exchange it for the armor of God, which is the person of Jesus!

What Do You Want Me to Do for You?

"So, Jesus answered and said to him, "What do you want Me to do for you? "The blind man said to Him, "Rabboni, that I may receive my sight." Then Jesus said to him, "Go your way; your faith has made you well." And immediately he received his sight and followed Jesus on the road."

In closing this meditation, let me say that Jesus heard Bartimaeus' cry for alignment. After being brought near, Jesus asked him, **"What do you want Me to do for you?" The blind man said, "Rabboni, I may receive my sight."**

I believe God is releasing prophetic vision and resetting our hearts, aligning them to His will so that we may **"follow Jesus on the road"** with a fresh anointing, a new fire, and a heart ignited with His glory! Neh'enah.

4

The Cry for Alignment! – Part 4

"And when Jesus was in Bethany at the house of Simon the leper, a woman came to Him having an alabaster flask of very costly fragrant oil, and she poured it on His head as He sat at the table. But when His disciples saw it, they were indignant, saying, "Why this waste? This fragrant oil might have been sold for much and given to the poor." But when Jesus was aware of it, He said to them, "Why do you trouble the woman? For she has done a good work for Me. For you have the poor with you always, but Me you do not have always. For in pouring this fragrant oil on My body, she did it for My burial. Assuredly, I say to you, wherever this gospel is preached in the whole world, what this woman has done will also be told as a memorial to her." (Matthew 26:6-13)

Allow me to bring up this one last portion about alignment.

The story above tells us of this one follower of Jesus who was burning inside to do this great thing to Christ, her Savior. After all, Jesus had been her all; Christ had set her free from a life of sin and corruption, and she now wanted to display her inner desire for what she truly felt for Him.

What is impressive to me is how people whom God has touched start strong in their devotion to Christ, but due to challenges in their lives, their love and passion for Jesus begin to wane, and their hearts grow cold and indifferent. It's not easy following Christ when the fire is gone!

Why the Fire Ceases

While I'm on this part of this devotion, let me add that following Jesus must be more than just an emotion birthed out of experiencing a miracle or the fulfillment of a promise. Following Christ must be much more profound than what meets the eye!

A believer's passion is mightily challenged when confronted with unfulfilled expectations. If we are not cautious, discouragement will set in when we don't see what we believe we should be seeing. Too often, this brings us out of alignment with God. Keep your eye on this and be on guard.

You see, our spirit longs to be aligned with God's Spirit. This is the call of His creation, to be aligned with Him. This is a word for all who call Jesus their Lord! Due to the countless negative things we will face in our walk, we will be challenged to stay aligned with God's desires.

Everything was perfect in the Garden of Eden. Man was connected and aligned with God until the serpent seduced him and fell out of alignment with God. After this, man was put out of the Garden and left without spirit, or perhaps his heart went dormant, and man was left to deal with life on their own. Being away from the Spirit of God means being away from the will of God. This is what it means not being aligned with God.

The woman in this story had been out of line with God, and now she had found a reason for living. Christ had brought her back to alignment with His will, and she couldn't help herself but give Christ her all, her most precious possession. What a beautiful place to be in! This should be our heart's desire daily.

When One Has Found Alignment with God!

After this servant discovered that Christ was at Simon the leper's house, she made her way there. She intended to pour this precious oil over the body of Jesus and anoint Him with it. Her most costly possession was about to be poured out on the Creator of the universe, upon Jesus the King of Glory! It didn't matter how expensive the oil was; it didn't matter who was present at Simon's house; nothing mattered to her but to align herself with God.

Interestingly, this woman didn't check in at the door. She didn't tell Judas, Peter, or Christ's disciples what she was about to do – she just did it! One thing I know about people passionate about Jesus is that they always flow against any current! Anything to release the longing for Jesus.

Here's what I'm thinking: Had she checked in at the door, the disciples might have told her what they said to her at the end after her deed of pouring oil was done, **"Why this waste? For this fragrant oil might have been sold for much and given to the poor."**

I do not intend to promote any rebellion, and I do believe in God's authority structure, but when it comes to pleasing Jesus, we must be extreme about pleasing His heart. This is my humble opinion.

When one longs to be aligned with God in worship and service, that individual will do all they can to get to that place of fulfillment. They will pray, fast, and spend their nights in tears in night watches; yes, they will not cease until they reach peace with themselves. This is what alignment with God is all about.

Often, God will anoint His servant to act, to enter a greater alignment, but the servant of God only goes so far and stops! He begins to doubt himself and then asks questions from fellow servants and friends. This is a real shame!

Note: Most people don't understand what God is doing in you – they can't help you. People will give you their opinions, ideas, etc.; eventually, they will change your mind from entering deeper alignment.

The goal is to release all God has placed in your heart; fire and passion are the keys to spiritual alignment. Learn to follow it! Neh'enah.

5

Too Tired to Pray!

"Then they came to a place which was named Gethsemane; and He said to His disciples, "Sit here while I pray." And He took Peter, James, and John with Him, and He began to be troubled and deeply distressed. Then He said to them, "My soul is exceedingly sorrowful, even to death. Stay here and watch." (Mark 14:32-34)

As I meditated upon this event in the life of Jesus at the Garden of Gethsemane, I got to thinking of several things:

The Privilege!

The first thing that came to my mind was how Christ had come to His hour of testing most brutally. He said, **"My soul is exceedingly sorrowful, even to death."** Have you ever been to a place where you could repeat these words? How deep was your sorrow? What was your outcome?

The second that struck me was that Peter, John, and James were invited to this experience. To see the Lord in greater fullness, in His hour of testing – is perhaps one of the most glorious experiences men could experience on earth. They were brought into a dimension that not too many had ever known. What a privilege!

Not What I Will!

"He went a little farther, and fell on the ground, and prayed that if it were possible, the hour might pass from Him. And He said, "Abba, Father, all things are possible for You. Take this cup away from Me; nevertheless, not what I will, but what You will." (Mark 14:35-36)

As Jesus pressed into prayer and poured His soul before the Father, Jesus made it very clear to the Father and said, **"Take this cup away from Me!"** In essence, Jesus was saying, I really don't want to go through this road, and if there is anything you can do, Father, to alter the course, I will gladly take that road instead. He was in an agony of spirit and soul. As soon as He made His request, He followed it up by saying, **"...nevertheless, not what I will, but what You will."** Jesus didn't back away from anything. He pressed into the Father's wishes. It was not about Him but about the Father's heart! This lesson He wanted to impart to His followers.

Wasted on Self!

"Then He came and found them sleeping and said to Peter, "Simon, are you sleeping? Could you not watch one hour? Watch and pray, lest you enter into temptation. The spirit indeed is willing, but the flesh is weak." (Mark 14:37-38)

As Jesus returns to check on the disciples, He discovers they are asleep. They were not even praying! No, sir, they had other things that occupied their being!

Way too often, believers convince themselves that they are followers of Christ simply because they attend a church gathering, go to a Bible study, or open their Bibles once a week. I wish I could applaud your belief in and philosophy of following Jesus.

You see, there are so-called "Christians" who are enamored with the externals of life. They stand and fall by them. When things go well for them, they say, Jesus is my Lord and King! When things go sour or nasty for them, they say, Life is complex, and the devil is after Me because I am that special. They live for an audience, not for Jesus!

The disciples discovered something they would never forget: the difference between life lived in the flesh and life lived in the spirit.

Walking in the Spirit, we are attentive to God's wishes. We do everything from His perspective. We consult Him for all matters in life that are life-altering. We spend time aligning our thoughts with His. We allow ourselves to be taught by His Word and continually pray for courage to fight the good fight of faith.

We are too occupied with our lives when we walk in the

flesh. We are too busy trying to figure out other people's lives when we can't make sense of ourselves. We waste ourselves on lesser things. We daily waste ourselves on ourselves! Our hearts, mind, strength, and soul are paralyzed for Jesus.

I believe the disciples couldn't pray for one hour with Jesus and accompany His restlessness of soul because their hearts were probably focused on the invitation, or who would make the grade to be the greatest, or who would be the one betraying Him, and many other mundane selfish thoughts. The point is that they fell asleep when they needed to be awake with Christ.

As I read this, I was reminded of myself and the countless times that I could not pray in the early morning hours because the night before, I wasted unnecessary time watching nonsense on the idiot box (television). They were all wasted on me! I had no strength; I did not fight for myself; I had no emotions to offer the Lord.

Left Speechless!

Finally, the things of earth leave us spiritually bankrupt with no emotions left in us to offer the Lord. The stuff of earth also leaves us empty with no real explanation to give our King for our lack of fight. Listen to this: **"Again He went away and prayed and spoke the same words. And when He returned, He found them asleep again, for their**

eyes were heavy, and they did not know what to answer Him." (Mark 14:39-40)

As I mentioned before, the life of the Spirit in Christ Jesus is the only way to keep ourselves in the flow of God. This life helps us stay in alignment with God's heart and mind. If we follow God with all our heart, mind, soul, and strength – we will watch and pray with Him! Neh'enah.

6

Only Believe!

"So, we departed from Horeb and went through all that great and terrible wilderness which you saw on the way to the mountains of the Amorites, as the LORD our God had commanded us. Then we came to Kadesh Barnea. And I said to you, 'You have come to the mountains of the Amorites, which the LORD our God is giving us. Look, the LORD your God has set the land before you; go up and possess it, as the LORD God of your fathers has spoken to you; do not fear or be discouraged.' "And every one of you came near to me and said, 'Let us send men before us, and let them search out the land for us, and bring back word to us of the way by which we should go up, and of the cities into which we shall come.' "The plan pleased me well; so I took twelve of your men, one man from each tribe. And they departed and went up into the mountains, and came to the Valley of Eschol, and spied it out. They also took some of the fruit of the land in their hands and brought it down to us; and they brought back word to us, saying, 'It is a good land which the LORD our God is giving us.' "Nevertheless, you would not go up, but rebelled against the command of the LORD your God; and you complained in your tents, and said, 'Because the LORD hates us, He has brought us out of the land of Egypt to deliver us into the hand of the Amorites, to destroy us. Where can we go up? Our brethren have discouraged our hearts, saying, "The people are greater and taller than we; the cities are great and fortified up to heaven; moreover we have seen the sons of the Anakim there." ' "Then I said to you, 'Do not be terrified or afraid of them. The LORD your God, who goes before you, He will fight for you, according to all He did for you in Egypt before your eyes, and in the wilderness where you saw how the LORD your God carried you, as a man carries his son, in all the way that you went until you came to this place.' Yet, for all that, you did not believe the LORD your God, who went in the way before you to search out a place for you to pitch your tents, to show you the way you should go, in the fire by night and in the cloud by day." (Deuteronomy 1: 19-33)

The Invitation!

During my early hours of prayer and meditation in God's word, the Spirit of the Lord caused my heart to receive fresh revelation about God's exchange with His people, Israel.

They had been walking towards the Promised Land, and it appears God had been leading them through the cloud by day and pillar of fire by night. God had been faithful and would continue to be precise if His people allowed Him to.

At Kadesh Barnea, they climbed the mountain of the Amorites and could see their future, the land of promise; yes, it was suitable before their eyes. What a wonder that must have been!

One thing to note here is that Israel not only saw the land of promise but was also challenged to possess it! Listen to this: **"Look, the LORD your God has set the land before you; go up and possess it, as the LORD God of your fathers has spoken to you; do not fear or be discouraged.'"** The children of Israel were under command, and God was sure to take them across and give them their promise, but they would have to face some enemies. Nothing had prepared them for what they would face as they took steps towards the promise – they would have to face the biggest enemy of all – self! No wonder Moses told them, **"...do not fear or be discouraged."**

The battle was not to be an external one but an internal one! Do you see this?

The Voice of Fear, Doubt, and Uncertainty

The plans of God are always perfect! He doesn't play games or tricks or plays peek-a-boo with us. When He says it is time to possess the land, He means it. He is not a man that He should lie, the Scripture says.

No sooner had the invitation to conquer come than a voice

out of nowhere started to speak. It was the voice of fear, doubt, and uncertainty! Instead of saying, "Yes and Amen, Lord – we will go," a negative vote in nature was raised. Listen to it: **"And every one of you came near to me and said, 'Let us send men before us, and let them search out the land for us, and bring back word to us of the way by which we should go up, and of the cities into which we shall come.'"**

Can you hear it?

The voice said, "We will go, but first, send men before us, and let them check out the land first!" This is fear in action! It is a voice that goes so deep into our hearts and minds and challenges the words of God spoken to us.

When people value themselves more than God or what God says, there will always be conflict when moving forward in God. The flesh doesn't like God's will and will not submit to it. The flesh must be brought under the government of God.

Here's what God decides to do after He hears their request:

God Opens the Veil!

"The plan pleased me well; so I took twelve of your men, one man from each tribe. And they departed and went up into the mountains, and came to the Valley of Eshcol,

and spied it out. They also took some of the fruit of the land in their hands and brought it down to us; and they brought back word to us, saying, 'It is a good land which the LORD our God is giving us.'"

It almost seems that the Lord went along with their wishes and consented to send spies into the Promised Land, one man from every tribe.

This means that God was not happy about their fear, but God would open the veil and allow His people to see what He was trying to prevent them from seeing. He initially wanted His people only to believe Him in His word, but they couldn't get themselves to do that. So, by His mercy, God sent the spies and allowed them to see the good, the bad, and the ugly and report back to all of them.

After the spies returned with the report, a decision had to be reached. Even after the news came back with great reviews, they didn't focus on the positive but on the negative. Overwhelmed by the possibility of dying at the hands of giants, the sons of Anakim concluded that it was best not to cross over!

Rebellion Prevails

"Nevertheless, you would not go up, but rebelled against the command of the LORD your God; and you complained in your tents, and said, 'Because the LORD

hates us, He has brought us out of the land of Egypt to deliver us into the hand of the Amorites, to destroy us. Where can we go up? Our brethren have discouraged our hearts, saying, "The people are greater and taller than we; the cities are great and fortified up to heaven; moreover, we have seen the sons of the Anakim there."

You and I will be tested by His Word alone. If we insist on seeing what is behind the veil, I believe God will show it to us, but I don't think it is His will to do this. He wants us to take His word at His word and trust Him.

After seeing the blessing and the giants, they felt they were not strong, intelligent, tall, and spiritual enough to overcome; thus, they gave up in their hearts.

God's Last Push!

Even though God's children expressed fear and doubt, God continued to pursue them by saying, **"... 'Do not be terrified or afraid of them. The LORD your God, who goes before you, He will fight for you, according to all He did for you in Egypt before your eyes, and in the wilderness where you saw how the LORD your God carried you, as a man carries his son, in all the way that you went until you came to this place.' Yet, for all that, you did not believe the LORD your God, who went in the way before you to search out a place for you to pitch your tents, to show you the way you should go, in the fire by night** and in the cloud by day."

In this passage, we see how good God is that He is willing to convince us by giving us a rundown of examples where He showed Himself strong on our behalf. Testimony after testimony of His faithfulness was revealed to Israel. God was not pleased with any of them except Caleb and Joshua. Yet, the flesh was way too strong to overcome.

Unbelief Aborts God's Plan

Nothing is more potent than unbelief. Without faith, it is impossible to please God, the Scripture says.

You see, God's works, the past miracles, were all powerful testimonies of His mercy. Yet, these were no match for a rebellious and fleshly heart! The outcome will be inevitable; spiritual abortion will be its result. No faith, no promise! Isn't this sad?

"You did not believe the Lord God..." (Deuteronomy 1:32).

What does the word believe mean in this context? Here's what I got: the word believe in Deuteronomy 1:32 means in its original Hebrew to confirm, to support. In other comments, God's children didn't know God enough to verify what He had said was true; they didn't know Him well enough to find support in Him or His words! Think about this.

Walking with God is about personal knowledge of Him; knowing Christ passionately and authentically is the key to advancement! Knowing Him more intimately is a must, not an option.

Only Believe

"Jesus answered them and said, "Most assuredly, I say to you, you seek Me, not because you saw the signs, but because you ate of the loaves and were filled. Do not labor for the food which perishes, but for the food which endures to everlasting life, which the Son of Man will give you, because God the Father has set His seal on Him." Then they said to Him, "What shall we do, that we may work the works of God?" Jesus answered and said to them, "This is the work of God, that you believe in Him whom He sent." (John 6:26-29)

In closing, let me share the value of this great principle.

In the days of Jesus, His disciples and other followers were amazed by the works of God. His miracles, the signs, and the wonders they experienced, without doubt, were mind-boggling. Jesus said, **"You seek Me, not because you saw the signs, but because you ate of the loaves and were filled. Do not labor for the food which perishes, but for food which endures to everlasting life, which the**

Son of Man will give you…".

To this, they replied, **"What shall we do, that we may work the works of God? "** **Jesus answered and said to them, "This is the work of God, that you believe in Him whom He sent."**

The flesh always looks for the externals of life. The spirit always looks for the Spirit, the internals. The people were looking at the works of God (external); Jesus said, **"This is the work of God, that you believe (internal)…."** Can you grasp this?

Believers who are still enslaved by the visible will always falter at this stage of their Christianity. We must ask God to reveal Himself in more extraordinary ways so that we may genuinely enter and behold the Lover of our souls as He is. Neh'enah.

7

When the Devil Wags His Head at You!

"And when they crucified Him, they divided His garments, casting lots for them to determine what every man should take. Now it was the third hour, and they crucified Him. And the inscription of His accusation was written above:
THE KING OF THE JEWS
They also crucified two robbers with Him, one on His right and the other on His left. So, the Scripture was fulfilled which says, "And He was numbered with the transgressors." And those who passed by blasphemed Him, wagging their heads and saying, "Aha! You who destroy the temple and build it in three days, save Yourself, and come down from the cross!" (Mark 15:24-30)

While in His presence this morning, the Lord opened my eyes to see these verses with greater understanding.

In serving God, I have learned how intense the battle is to stay in rhythm with God's order and design. The temptation to go faster or slower (in life in general) than what He demands has never been greater, yet the disciplined vessel of God must dig deep in His soul and be ever so attentive to God's voice to stay in the fight.

Along with hearing and obeying God in daily life, we have other battles, such as the demonic voice from the devil himself, challenging every thought, every past failure, every move or course of action, and every decision to continue pursuing God's heart.

As you know, the devil hates Jesus and everything He stands for. But He doesn't stop there. Since he can't hurt Jesus anymore, he attacks His body, that is, you and me, His servants.

The more we as a church set ourselves to cause damage to his kingdom of darkness, the more he releases an array of schemes, tricks, and set-ups against us! We must realize this quickly.

Of all the many things the devil attacks, I want to address a few things he pursued in Jesus's life. Christ is our model, and just as the enemy dealt with Christ, we will be handled like that.

The Scripture in Mark says that after Jesus was hanging on the cross, **"...those who passed by blasphemed Him, wagging their heads and saying, "Aha! You who destroy the temple and build it in three days, save Yourself, and come down from the cross!"**

It is evident from the text that the enemy hated Jesus with a passion. The devil wanted Him dead and would do his best to embarrass and demoralize him as much as possible before he eventually kills him.

When the devil saw Jesus hanging on that cross, he would wag his head at Him and say, save yourself. This is precisely what the devil thinks of us – when we give our all for Jesus.

Here's what the devil wags his ugly head at:

First, the devil wags his head at your obedience to God. When the devil looks at us obeying God at any cost to do His will, he mocks and ridicules us for not following our fleshly dreams.

Let this mind be in you which was also in Christ Jesus, who, being in the form of God, did not consider it robbery to be equal with God, but made Himself of no reputation, taking the form of a bondservant, and coming in the likeness of men. And being found in appearance as a man, He humbled Himself and became obedient to the point of death, even the death of the cross." (Philippians 2:5-8)

Only faithful servants can take orders from heaven. You can't be a servant when you think you are a king! Unless you are willing to make **"yourself of no reputation,"** it will be tough for you to become obedient to the will of God.

The enemy knows our fleshly desires and tries to keep us entwined and engaged in them. He will always tempt us with our desires. He will try to avoid God's will by offering substitutes. Substitutes only keep us wasting time. They make our flesh gloat and expand. People pat us on the back and say, "Keep going, brother. You are doing well!" This keeps us temporarily encouraged, but we are nowhere near God's plan for our lives.

One of my mentors used to say to me, "David, when a man begins to backslide in his heart, the first thing he does is he goes back to the last wicked stronghold he was under bondage to!"

The second thing the devil wags his ugly head at is our passion for God.

"Therefore we also, since we are surrounded by so great a cloud of witnesses, let us lay aside every weight, and the sin which so easily ensnares us, and let us run with endurance the race that is set before us, looking unto Jesus, the author and finisher of our faith, who for the joy that was set before Him endured the cross, despising the shame, and has sat down at the right hand of the throne of God." (Hebrews 12:1, 2)

The devil hates passionate lovers of Jesus. The devil will always praise the flesh at work. People get excited about emotional breakthroughs. Let me tell you: Our emotions are like rollercoasters – they will go up and down. Some people's joy depends on whether they get a promotion or a raise at work. These fleshly attitudes don't make the devil "wag" his head. Instead, he claps, rejoices with you, and joins the fun! When Jesus is no longer your fire, you will warm yourself with another's fire! Just like Peter did when he betrayed the Lord.

When a man or woman of God is passionate about Him and His will, they are unstoppable. They are people who have caught a glimpse of the world to come. They are not content with just getting by. They are not living for the pleasure of a man or trying to be the biggest this or that. They are caught up with something much bigger than themselves: they are caught up in the glory of the great I AM!

Lastly, the devil will wag his head at your commitment to God!

"When He had been baptized, Jesus came up immediately from the water, and behold, the heavens were opened to Him, and He saw the Spirit of God descending like a dove and alighting upon Him. And suddenly a voice came from heaven, saying, "This is My beloved Son, in whom I am well pleased." Then Jesus was led up by the Spirit into the wilderness to be tempted by the devil. And when He had fasted forty days and forty nights…". (Matthew 3:16-4:2)

You can think of over a million reasons for not being at the place you are now. You don't have to pray; you don't have to read your Bible; you don't have to be a testimony to people at work, at home, etc. You don't even have to be here at this place of worship. You can quit the whole thing, and no one will care.

So, the devil makes his move in telling you to associate with the people at church and play the part. Still, you don't need to commit yourself to sacrifice to have this crazy passion for God, and you don't need to embarrass yourself in front of people who don't care to hear about Jesus! Just buy the Christian T-shirt and cap and let everybody see what a witness you are for Jesus. Just be yourself! Be Christian in name only; you don't need to fast and pray, you don't have to get rid of your pet sins, you don't need to be baptized in fire, you don't need indwelling, you don't need anointing, you don't need any of this nonsense!"

One of my mentors used to say; You will always have to fight for the right way to live!

When the devil saw Jesus coming into the wilderness right out of His baptism at the Jordan in Matthew 4, he knew well that Jesus was now under the Father's government. He was not just a man who wanted to please the Father; He knew Jesus was a Man on a mission!

Great Is Your Reward!

"Blessed are you when they revile and persecute you, and falsely say all kinds of evil against you for My sake. Rejoice and be exceedingly glad, for great is your reward in heaven, for so they persecuted the prophets who were before you." (Matthew 5:11-13)

As I close these thoughts, I want you to know that God will always favor those who favor Him.

My friends, let us settle this once and for all: So, what if the devil is mocking, ridiculing, reviling, and wagging his ugly head at you? If you know you have sinned, repent; then run back to God and drop at His feet as fast as possible.

If we walk in repentance and brokenness - God will always sustain us! Learn to please the Father and trust me; God will uphold us despite persecution and mockery. Neh'enah.

The Heart of David Journal

8

Unlimited Fire!

"Now in the sixth month, the angel Gabriel was sent by God to a city of Galilee named Nazareth, to a virgin betrothed to a man whose name was Joseph, of the house of David. The virgin's name was Mary. And having come in, the angel said to her, "Rejoice, highly favored one, the Lord is with you; blessed are you among women!" But when she saw him, she was troubled at his saying and considered what manner of greeting this was. Then the angel said to her, "Do not be afraid, Mary, for you have found favor with God. And behold, you will conceive in your womb and bring forth a Son and shall call His name JESUS. He will be great and will be called the Son of the Highest, and the Lord God will give Him the throne of His Father David. And He will reign over the house of Jacob forever, and of His kingdom, there will be no end." Then Mary said to the angel, "How can this be since I do not know a man?" And the angel answered and said to her, "The Holy Spirit will come upon you, and the power of the Highest will overshadow you; therefore, also, that Holy One who is to be born will be called the Son of God. Now indeed, Elizabeth your relative has also conceived a son in her old age; and this is now the sixth month for her who was called barren. For with God, nothing will be impossible." Then Mary said,

"Behold the maidservant of the Lord! Let it be to me according to your word." And the angel departed from her." (Luke 1:26-38)

Is it Consecration or Probation unto the Lord?

When I think of Mary, who was a virgin and had set herself apart from her youth to be espoused to Joseph, I think of divine order for her life. To be set apart and to wait for marriage to become intimate with a man speaks of God's pattern for life.

This also marks a fascinating pattern of how God prepares His vessels for His use.

I don't believe Mary was looking for anything spiritual to come her way or for her to be noted and marked by an angel as **"a highly favored among women"** comment. She wasn't living in preparation for anything but only to fall in love and marry Joseph.

Earth never took note of her lifestyle, but Heaven did! The Lord had her eyes on her for as long as she had lived.

As we live before God, we must always be conscious of His workings. People might not be looking or even care about us, but know that God has you and me under probation!

A Visitation from God

After the angel Gabriel gave Mary a warm greeting and declared to her how God felt about her, he proceeded to say, **"...you will conceive in your womb and bring forth a Son and shall call His name JESUS."**

It was the angel's way of saying, "God wants to deposit in your womb an expression from heaven; His name is Jesus. He desires to impregnate you with divine life! God longs to bring forth a Son!"

God's intention was to be expressed through a willing vessel. We must note that God was not looking for exceptional talent, unique ability, or some certificate qualifying her for the job. No sir! All God needed from Mary was her womb, which speaks to us of her willingness, nothing else.

For those called to serve Him, you know it wasn't your beauty, talent, or gift that God looked at when He chose you. It was your heart, your spiritual womb! It always is about our spiritual womb.

We never really know the potential hidden behind what God is about to do in us. Much of that potential is based upon our obedience and how far we are willing to follow. The angel told Mary that what would happen to her was immense. Listen to this prophetic promise: **"He will be great and will be called the Son of the Highest; and the**

Lord God will give Him the throne of His father David. And He will reign over the house of Jacob forever, and of His kingdom there will be no end." Some of the stuff God has in store for some of us has generational consequences. Whether big or small, it's about obedience and lending ourselves to the Lord for His use.

How Can This Be?

"Then Mary said to the angel, "How can this be, since I do not know a man?"
The question of the ages for all of us who believe in Christ and long to be used by God has always been the same, "How can this be?
Mary quickly said, "I do not know a man!"

Too often, we look at what we don't have, what we don't feel, what we can or can't do, or what others have said…. and without God's discernment, we conclude, *This can't happen in me or to me or through me!* We have all been guilty of putting our trust in self to bring about a true expression of Jesus! This is where man stops, and God begins.

Maybe according to man's standards or in man's eyes, we have gained wealth, status, a reputation, etc. What does that have to do with God's divine order? If you allow the fire of God to come upon you, it will consume all of this! All of it.

When we allow our flesh to control our lives, we will become corrupt. The flesh only knows to sin; it doesn't know anything else. To think that creating with your hands what you have lost in your soul is the best thing to do, you are setting yourself up for heartbreaks!

When the Anointing Comes!

"And the angel answered and said to her, "The Holy Spirit will come upon you, and the power of the Highest will overshadow you; therefore, also, that Holy One who is to be born will be called the Son of God."

The work of God is done in us by the Holy Spirit. It was never intended for man to do God's will alone by His power. What seemed impossible for Mary was quickly put to rest when the angel said, **"The Holy Spirit will come upon you, and the power of the Highest will overshadow you…"**

The Holy Spirit coming upon means figuratively to come on someone; thus, a stronger comes on the weaker. The Holy Spirit, represented as the power of God, comes on men whom God blesses. [Theological Dictionary of the New Testament (electronic ed., Vol. 2, p. 681). Eerdmans.] Also, to be overshadowed by the power of the Highest means, the capacity of God, or the ability or enabling of God, will come over you like a shadow. She was covered in capacity, if you will. In other words, God will do the impossible and Ask Mary to lend her womb by willful choice.

To make his point, the angel Gabriel testifies to Elizabeth's impregnation, denoting that she was barren, and states, **"For with God nothing will be impossible."**

The issue has never been whether God is able; we know He is. The problem is found in man's ability to take heed, in being quick to hear and obey. Once God speaks, man is left with a decision. It will be yes, yes, or no, no!

Mary Sets History in Motion

"Then Mary said, "Behold the maidservant of the Lord! Let it be to me according to your word."

Everything was placed on hold until Mary allowed God to flow into and through her. It will be the same with you and me.

Unlimited fire is found when we allow God to move in us, not before! There must be a willingness to surrender, obey, and be led by God's anointing – by His Spirit! Neh'enah.

9

Learn to Follow the Promise!

"Therefore, you shall keep every commandment which I command you today, that you may be strong, and go in and possess the land which you cross over to possess, and that you may prolong your days in the land which the LORD swore to give your fathers, to them and their descendants, 'a land flowing with milk and honey.' For the land which you go to possess is not like the land of Egypt from which you have come, where you sowed your seed and watered it by foot, as a vegetable garden; but the land which you cross over to possess is a land of hills and valleys, which drinks water from the rain of heaven, a land for which the LORD your God cares; the eyes of the LORD your God are always on it, from the beginning of the year to the very end of the year. 'And it shall be that if you earnestly obey My commandments which I command you today, to love the LORD your God and serve Him with all your heart and with all your soul, then I will give you the rain for your land in its season, the early rain and the latter rain, that you may gather in your grain, your new wine, and your oil." (Deuteronomy 11:8-14)

As I read this portion of the Word of God, I couldn't help but notice how the Lord makes a world of distinction between the land of Egypt and His promised land. You would think land is land, and there is no difference, so what makes the difference?

It is my conviction, as the Holy Spirit opened my spiritual understanding, that wherever the Lord leads and wherever the Lord lays His hand, this is holy ground, this is a land of blessing and favor and promise!

Let's dive in and discover the fantastic leadership of the Holy Spirit as He shows us the ways of the Lord more accurately.

It's All About the Commandments!

"Therefore, you shall keep every commandment which I command you today, that you may be strong, and go in and possess the land which you cross over to possess, and that you may prolong your days in the land which the LORD swore to give your fathers, to them and their descendants, 'a land flowing with milk and honey.'

One thing we must learn about God and God's people is that they are constantly under marching orders. They don't have a curriculum for life. God has left an instructional manual to follow. This is a fact. It's called the Holy Bible, the Word of God.

Now, some people have chosen to opt out of this. They

have created their manual on how to live and prosper, etc. As good as their manual is, it is not God's Word(s). There are no warranties or guarantees when we do things by ourselves. I'm just saying.

So, the Holy Spirit, through the hands of Moses, wrote a love letter to God's people and told them to keep every commandment that God commanded them. This was the key to their success in crossing the Jordan and establishing a lasting future in the Promised Land. The victory was all about keeping the commandments of God.

His Guarantee!

"For the land which you go to possess is not like the land of Egypt from which you have come, where you sowed your seed and watered it by foot, as a vegetable garden; but the land which you cross over to possess is a land of hills and valleys, which drinks water from the rain of heaven, a land for which the LORD your God cares; the eyes of the LORD your God are always on it, from the beginning of the year to the very end of the year."

Moses continued his discourse with God's people and told them where they were, meaning Egypt, the land they came from, was very different from where they were headed. It was a world of difference – because God would be in it!

In the fields of Egypt, they had to sow the seed and water

it themselves. They had to plant their vegetable gardens, etc. The comparison came when God, through Moses, said, **"The land which you cross over to possess is a land of hills and valleys, which drinks water from the rain of heaven, a land for which the Lord your God cares."** Moses adds, **"The eyes of the Lord your God are always on it, from the beginning of the year to the very end of the year."**

How can anyone lose with God? would be my initial thought. How can anyone whine due to misfortune in God? It will never happen!

To follow the Lord into His promise in any area of our lives is a sure guarantee that His eyes will be upon it, caring for every move we make in Him! A guarantee! This is what we get if we follow Him fully.

The Rainmakers!

"And it shall be that if you earnestly obey My commandments which I command you today, to love the LORD your God and serve Him with all your heart and with all your soul, then I will give you the rain for your land in its season, the early rain and the latter rain, that you may gather in your grain, your new wine, and your oil."

Earnest obedience to love God and serve Him with all the heart and soul makes the rain descend. It will happen for any soul who walks in humility, any church that humbles itself, and our nation if we humble ourselves before God.

An obstacle may come to us as disobedience or impatience to await the Lord's instruction. Our peers may pressure us to act, but we must wait, knowing God only blesses what or where He commissions. Our flesh might want to run when God is saying wait.

If we wait, we will experience His provision in any place He desires to lead us. If He is not leading, we will face an endless uphill climb! Neh'enah.

10

Rules to Follow When Pregnant with God!

"And it came to pass in those days that a decree went out from Caesar Augustus that all the world should be registered. This census first took place while Quirinius was governing Syria. So, all went to be registered, everyone to his city. Joseph also went up from Galilee, out of the city of Nazareth, into Judea, to the city of David, which is called Bethlehem, because he was of the house and lineage of David, to be registered with Mary, his betrothed wife, who was with child. So it was, that while they were there, the days were completed for her to be delivered. And she brought forth her firstborn Son, and wrapped Him in swaddling clothes, and laid Him in a manger because there was no room for them in the inn." (Luke 2:1-7)

Who Was with Child!

For the most part, we have all heard the Christmas story and the announcement made by the angel Gabriel to Mary regarding the birthing of Jesus. Here is a woman who is still puzzled from that one encounter with the angel Gabriel she has been carrying in her womb for the last nine months, Jesus Christ our Savior.

Being impregnated by the Spirit of God must be one of the most exciting and anticipating moments in a believer's life. Too many believers don't understand the workings of God in their lives, and due to their lack of understanding, they abort what God may have for their lives.

I have seen the Holy Spirit touch believers, and due to their lack of understanding and discipline, they never fully entered God's call on their lives. How do I know this to be accurate? Well, for the simple reason that I have also seen it in my own life, not just once but countless times.

In this story, let me show you what I believe God is saying to our spirit.

While the world turned in the life of Joseph and Mary, they carried the promised Son Jesus in their womb. We must always be conscious that both worlds (the spiritual and the natural) are happening simultaneously. The earth sees one thing, and heaven sees another.

During this time, Caesar Augustus decreed a census, and everyone had to register in their city. I can only imagine the difficulty of getting Mary out to go and write because she was about to give birth to Christ. So, Joseph and Mary headed to their respective place to register.

When One is Pregnant with God . . .

Now, there are things that one must realize and put into practice when God has commissioned them.

Just because the Lord has chosen one doesn't exempt us from keeping with governmental and civic responsibilities. One must attend to one's civic duties as part of belonging to a system of government. Too many people will oust themselves from the earth per se and say, God has called me, and I don't need to comply with the governmental structure. Some cults and religions do this. This would be rebellion against the government, and by the way, God instituted this.

Another thing we find is that when God wants to begin moving through us, we must be ready. Mary didn't know she would give birth to Jesus right before her census registration! It was the Lord's time, and she had to be ready and find a place to give birth.

The story of Christ's birth tells us there was no room in the inn. There was no room anywhere to give birth to Jesus! Mary had to do what she had to and release the baby, for the time had come. So, she did what any responsible servant of God would do – she found a manger in a stable, yes, in a barn! Christ was born in a stable.

Small Beginnings is Foundational to the Process!

When called or commissioned by God with a purpose, one

must be ready to start when God's gun goes off. He is not asking me if I am ready – I should always be prepared! I don't need resources; I need Him. I don't need man's approval; I only need to hear Him say, "Go!"

The rule for the man or woman of God who has been impregnated with God is always to begin with what you have and start when the Holy Ghost tells you, "Go!" To obey His voice is to set in motion all heaven in your favor. As I close this meditation, be attentive to the Holy Spirit's call to run with the vision! Neh'enah.

11

Impartation of Life!

"In the year that King Uzziah died, I saw the Lord sitting on a throne, high and lifted up, and the train of His robe filled the temple. Above it stood seraphim; each one had six wings: with two he covered his face, with two he covered his feet, and with two he flew. And one cried to another and said:
"Holy, holy, holy is the LORD of hosts;
The whole earth is full of His glory!"
And the posts of the door were shaken by the voice of him who cried out, and the house was filled with smoke. So I said:
"Woe is me, for I am undone!
Because I am a man of unclean lips,
And I dwell in the midst of a people of unclean lips;
For my eyes have seen the King,
The LORD of hosts."
Then one of the seraphim flew to me, having in his hand a live coal which he had taken with the tongs from the altar. And he touched my mouth with it, and said:
"Behold, this has touched your lips;
Your iniquity is taken away,
And your sin purged."
Also I heard the voice of the Lord, saying:
"Whom shall I send,

And who will go for Us?"
Then I said, "Here am I! Send me." (Isaiah 6:1-8)

A Life Established!

I know little about Isaiah's life except what commentaries and Bible dictionaries say about this powerful and prophetic servant of the Lord. Knowing that the prophet Isaiah was family to King Uzziah would be very interesting.

Listen to this: According to tradition, his father, Amos, and King Amaziah of Judah were brothers (Megillah 10b), making Isaiah and Amaziah's son King Uzziah first cousins. Isaiah's activities and influence were at their peak during the reign of King Hezekiah, Uzziah's great-grandson.

Some scholars reveal that perhaps Isaiah was in a good place when King Uzziah was around, and there was no need to depend upon the Lord. This would not be stretching any truth. Many of us have the fleshly tendency not to go after the Lord when things are going well. It is such an obvious thing to see in God's people today.

When King Uzziah Died

"In the year that King Uzziah died, I saw the Lord sitting on a throne... "

I believe many things will change if we truly understand

the heart of Jesus right now. Many things must end in us before we can see the Lord! Let me add that unless there is death first, there can't be any life.

We want more of Jesus in our hearts, but in our minds, we want Him to fit into our selfish agendas. How foolish we, His servants, have become currently! We want God to come and invade our preconceived mindset, to impregnate us with the seed of His glory when we have not provided a spiritual womb for birthing.

We want passion, zeal, power, and fire, but we don't want to die to ourselves!

Unless the Seed Dies!

In John 14:24, the seed dying and being changed into a different form occurs. Jesus said, **"If the seed doesn't die, it abides alone, but if it dies, it bears much fruit."**

If I can't see my selfishness, good works, contacts, status, and good reputation as in the way of God moving, then I am, of most men, to be pitied! Unless we die, we won't see God; we will not experience the fire of God!

When God calls a man, you must know He calls him to die first. Know that death is a prerequisite for God's fire to descend upon you.

My Call to Die!

I came into the kingdom of God by God's mercy in the late 1980s, and it wasn't long before I received my call to follow Jesus.

Sunday evening services were popular back then, and missionaries used to be invited to speak at our church. I wasn't a fan of going to church on Sunday nights, so my wife and I would hardly, if ever, attend them.

My pastor came to me one Sunday morning and invited me to attend the upcoming Sunday evening service, and only because he asked us to come to it, we did, otherwise, we would not have come to it. God knew my heart and knew I was uninterested in hearing any missionary speak. Yet, to honor my pastor, I came. My life entered a spiritual revolution here that I will never forget.

The more the missionary spoke, the angrier I became. It wasn't what he said that got me that way; it was the working of God's Spirit in my heart, almost like a war between my soul and spirit.

That night, when we came home, I soon went to sleep. At about 3 a.m., the Lord gave me a dream. Jesus visited me in the dream and took and showed me a blueprint. After showing me all this, He brought me back to the original place where I was standing before He picked me up. After that dream, I couldn't go to sleep. So, I got up to pray. As I prayed, I had a vision. I saw my dream replay on the wall. I had a vision of God.

During my conversation with Jesus, He called me to serve Him all my life. I had too many reservations and was having a hard time surrendering. I finally did. As soon as I said, "Yes, Lord, send me!" He anointed my life to serve Him.

I learned that I was imparted His life as soon as I died to myself. It has been over 35 years, and I feel that fire as fresh tonight as I felt it that night when He visited me.
As I close, let me add this: Unless we surrender our hearts and die, we won't see what He wants us to see. Neh'enah.

12

Where Did the Fire Go?

"Then the LORD spoke to Moses, saying, "Command Aaron and his sons, saying, 'This is the law of the burnt offering: The burnt offering shall be on the hearth upon the altar all night until morning, and the fire of the altar shall be kept burning on it. And the priest shall put on his linen garment and his linen trousers he shall put on his body and take up the ashes of the burnt offering which the fire has consumed on the altar, and he shall put them beside the altar. Then he shall take off his garments, put on other garments, and carry the ashes outside the camp to a clean place. And the fire on the altar shall be kept burning on it; it shall not be put out. And the priest shall burn wood on it every morning and lay the burnt offering in order on it and he shall burn on it the fat of the peace offerings. A fire shall always be burning on the altar; it shall never go out." (Leviticus 6:8-13)

God required fire to be set upon the altar. The priests were commanded to have a fire burning all day and all night, and from reading the Scriptures, the priests lived this way. They were present, and the fire was burning as the Lord commanded.

Let me rephrase: It is possible to live in this world without fire, but we have been left without options for those who seek to be apostolic servants of God. We could not live without fire in such a dark, cold, and complicated world. We must have the fire.

When Fire Begins to Die!

"Now the boy Samuel ministered to the LORD before Eli. And the word of the LORD was rare in those days; there was no widespread revelation. And it came to pass at that time, while Eli was lying down in his place, and when his eyes had begun to grow so dim that he could not see, and before the lamp of God went out in the tabernacle of the LORD where the ark of God was, and while Samuel was lying down, that the LORD called Samuel." (1 Samuel 3:1-3)

When God's fire begins to run low, the first thing we lose is our discernment. Our perception of God becomes cloudy, and our lives and leadership begin to reflect the dullness of spirit.

Then the LORD said to Samuel: "Behold, I will do something in Israel at which both ears of everyone who hears it will tingle. On that day, I will perform against Eli all that I have spoken concerning his house, from beginning to end. For I have told him that I will judge his house forever for the iniquity which he knows, because his sons made themselves vile, and he did not restrain

them. And therefore, I have sworn to the house of Eli that the iniquity of Eli's house shall not be atoned for by sacrifice or offering forever." (1 Samuel 3:11-14)

When the fire of God is gone, the first step downward is that we lose favor with God. Our life becomes dry and indifferent. We run programs and fleshly ideas to keep the "ball rolling." Yet, deep inside, you know that something is missing; something has been lost.

Outwardly, things still look fine. People still respect us somewhat, and the ministry continues with its momentum, but something needs to be added and recovered.

The Consequence of Having No Fire!

It wasn't long before the loss of fire would take effect, and what was internally missing would be made manifest. Listen: **"Now Israel went out to battle against the Philistines and encamped beside Ebenezer, and the Philistines encamped in Aphek. Then the Philistines put themselves in battle array against Israel. And when they joined battle, Israel was defeated by the Philistines, who killed about four thousand men of the army in the field. And when the people had come into the camp, the elders of Israel said, "Why has the LORD defeated us today before the Philistines?**

The time came for another battle against the Philistines,

and the Israelites took their place. I mean, they were ready to fight (without God.). When we begin to experience inevitable defeats, it would be wise to ask ourselves, "Why do I feel like I'm doing something wrong?"

One elder of Israel spoke out and said, **"Why has the Lord defeated us today before the Philistine?"** Notice that the elder didn't say, "Why has the Philistines, the devil, or the enemy... defeated us today? He said the Lord had beaten us.

When His Presence Becomes a Lucky Charm!

Let us bring the ark of the covenant of the LORD from Shiloh to us, that when it comes among us, it may save us from the hand of our enemies." So, the people sent to Shiloh, that they might bring from there the ark of the covenant of the LORD of hosts, who dwells between the cherubim. And the two sons of Eli, Hophni and Phinehas, were there with the ark of the covenant of God. And when the ark of the covenant of the LORD came into the camp, all Israel shouted so loudly that the earth shook. Now when the Philistines heard the noise of the shout, they said, "What does the sound of this great shout in the camp of the Hebrews mean?" Then, they understood that the ark of the LORD had come into the camp. So the Philistines were afraid, for they said, "God has come into the camp!" And they said, "Woe to us! For such a thing has never happened before. Woe to us! Who will deliver

us from the hand of these mighty gods? These are the gods who struck the Egyptians with all the plagues in the wilderness. Be strong and conduct yourselves like men, you Philistines, that you do not become servants of the Hebrews, as they have been to you. Conduct yourselves like men and fight!" So, the Philistines fought, and Israel was defeated, and every man fled to his tent. There was a very great slaughter, and there fell of Israel's thirty-thousand-foot soldiers. Also, the ark of God was captured, and the two sons of Eli, Hophni, and Phinehas, died.

Then, a man named Benjamin ran from the battle line the same day and came to Shiloh with his clothes torn and dirt on his head. Now, when he came, there was Eli, sitting on a seat by the wayside watching, for his heart trembled for the ark of God. And when the man came into the city and told it, all the city cried out. When Eli heard the noise of the outcry, he said, "What does the sound of this tumult mean?" And the man came quickly and told Eli. Eli was ninety-eight years old, and his eyes were so dim that he could not see. Then the man said to Eli, "I am he who came from the battle. And I fled today from the battle line."

And he said, "What happened, my son?"

So, the messenger answered and said, "Israel has fled before the Philistines, and there has been a great slaughter among the people. Also, your two sons, Hophni and Phinehas, are dead, and the ark of God has been captured."

Then it happened, when he made mention of the ark of God, that Eli fell off the seat backward by the side of the gate; and his neck was broken and he died, for the man was old and heavy. And he had judged Israel forty years. Now his daughter-in-law, Phinehas' wife, was with child, due to be delivered, and when she heard the news that the ark of God was captured and that her father-in-law and her husband were dead, she bowed herself and gave birth, for her labor pains came upon her. And about the time of her death, the women who stood by her said to her, "Do not fear, for you have borne a son." But she did not answer, nor did she regard it. Then she named the child Ichabod, saying, "The glory has departed from Israel!" because the ark of God had been captured and because of her father-in-law and her husband. And she said, "The glory has departed from Israel, for the ark of God has been captured." (1 Samuel 4:1-22)

As we follow the battle, God had intended for all of Israel to be humbled. He allowed the enemy to embarrass His people and expose their pride and self!

I have heard people say God is a good God, and He won't allow the enemy to have His way. My friends, it is not the enemy that God is concerned with; His people have lost the fire because of sin and compromise. His people have gone the opposite of what God had initially intended. Isn't this always the case?

God's people felt that if they could bring the ark of the covenant, which is symbolic of the presence of God, they would be able to send the enemy running. In most cases, God's presence was active, but not this time. God had removed His hand and was no longer in their midst.

My friends, if you hear His voice today, there is a reason for much of what we face today. I know it to be accurate; I have lived this and experienced the dreadfulness of not walking in His presence.

Listen: The ark of God isn't going to save you when there is rebellion in the heart, and the fire of God will not burn by a simple prayer. It's going to take much more than that. It's going to take a repentant and contrite spirit before God. Let us humble ourselves in His presence. Neh'enah.

13

Fresh Fire!

There is an old hymn my pastor would often share with me:

Thou Christ of burning, cleansing flame,
Send the fire, send the fire, send the fire!
Thy blood-bought gift today, we claim,
Send the fire, send the fire, send the fire!
Look down and see this waiting host,
Give us the promised Holy Ghost;
We want another Pentecost,
Send the fire, send the fire, send the fire!

God of Elijah, hear our cry:
Send the fire, send the fire, send the fire!
To make us fit to live or die,
Send the fire, send the fire, send the fire!
To burn up every trace of sin,
To bring the light and glory in,
The revolution now begin,
Send the fire, send the fire, send the fire!

'Tis fire we want, for fire we plead,
Send the fire, send the fire, send the fire!
The fire will meet our every need,

David Mayorga

Send the fire, send the fire, send the fire!
For strength to ever do the right,
For grace to conquer in the fight,
For pow'r to walk the world in white,
Send the fire, send the fire, send the fire!

To make our weak hearts strong and brave,
Send the fire, send the fire, send the fire!
To live a dying world to save,
Send the fire, send the fire, send the fire!
Oh, see us on Thy altar lay
Our lives, our all, this very day;
To crown the off'ring now we pray,
Send the fire, send the fire, send the fire!
- William Booth (1829-1912)

"So, Ahab sent for all the children of Israel and gathered the prophets together on Mount Carmel. And Elijah came to all the people, and said, "How long will you falter between two opinions? If the LORD is God, follow Him; but if Baal, follow him." But the people answered him not a word. Then Elijah said to the people, "I alone am left a prophet of the LORD, but Baal's prophets are four hundred and fifty men. Therefore, let them give us two bulls; and let them choose one bull for themselves, cut it in pieces, and lay it on the wood, but put no fire under it; and I will prepare the other bull, and lay it on the wood, but put no fire under it. Then you call on the name of your gods, and I will call on the name of the LORD;

and the God who answers by fire, He is God."

So all the people answered and said, "It is well-spoken."

Now Elijah said to the prophets of Baal, "Choose one bull for yourselves and prepare it first, for you are many; and call on the name of your god but put no fire under it."

So they took the bull which was given them, and they prepared it, and called on the name of Baal from morning even till noon, saying, "O Baal, hear us!" But there was no voice; no one answered. Then they leaped about the altar which they had made.

And so it was, at noon, that Elijah mocked them and said, "Cry aloud, for he is a god; either he is meditating, or he is busy, or he is on a journey, or perhaps he is sleeping and must be awakened." So, they cried aloud, and cut themselves, as was their custom, with knives and lances, until the blood gushed out on them. And when midday was past, they prophesied until the time of the offering of the evening sacrifice. But there was no voice; no one answered, no one paid attention.
Then Elijah said to all the people, "Come near to me." So, all the people came near to him. And he repaired the broken altar of the Lord. And Elijah took twelve stones, according to the number of the tribes of the sons of Jacob, to whom the word of the LORD had come, saying,

"Israel shall be your name." Then, with the stones he built an altar in the name of the LORD; and he made a trench around the altar large enough to hold two seahs of seed. And he put the wood in order, cut the bull in pieces, and laid it on the wood, and said, "Fill four waterpots with water, and pour it on the burnt sacrifice and on the wood." Then he said, "Do it a second time," and they did it a second time; and he said, "Do it a third time," and they did it a third time. So the water ran all around the altar, and he also filled the trench with water.

And it came to pass, at the time of the offering of the evening sacrifice, that Elijah the prophet came near and said, "LORD God of Abraham, Isaac, and Israel, let it be known this day that You are God in Israel, and I am Your servant, and that I have done all these things at Your word. Hear me, O LORD, hear me, that this people may know that You are the LORD God and that You have turned their hearts back to You again."

Then the fire of the LORD fell and consumed the burnt sacrifice, and the wood and the stones and the dust, and it licked up the water that was in the trench. Now when all the people saw it, they fell on their faces; and they said, "The LORD, He is God! The LORD, He is God!" (1 Kings 18:20-40)

The Intention to Meet God!

Experiencing God is not as easy as some teach. Experiencing God must be intentional for the most part.

Before we can experience God in greater fullness, especially for those who know the Lord, we must learn some of the things required. Elijah teaches us this in 1 Kings 18.

    1. The Repairing of the altar. Nothing is more challenging for a man or woman of God than to confess that they have grown weary, cold, and indifferent. To evaluate oneself, one has to be the most prominent personal mountain to climb in faith. Unless we admit we are not where we know God wants us to be, we will never grow an appetite for His presence, purpose, and power!

    2. The Twelve Stones. Symbolized divine order. We must come to where we want to be aligned with God. It is the alignment that says, "Nothing will fill my heart but the fire of His presence burning and leading me in the way!" It was Elijah's way of showing a rededication to God. Remember, revival starts within!

    3. Put wood in order & pieces of bull. This speaks of obedience to what God is demanding. This is doing what we do in the natural. We are preparing for something to come from heaven. We don't know what God has in store, but we are doing what we know to do.

    4. Fill 4 Waterpots. Water is a symbol of the Holy

Ghost. There is pleading and crying for God to come by His Spirit, and we will not cease until the fire falls!

I don't know where you are with God currently. Only you know. I believe that if the fire is what you are pleading and contending for, God will meet you as you open your spirit to Him. Neh'enah.

14

Get Alone and Wait for Fire!

"Tarry and wait for the promise of the Father...." (Luke 24:49)

"When the Day of Pentecost had fully come, they were all with one accord in one place. And suddenly, a sound from heaven, like a mighty rushing wind, filled the whole house where they were sitting. Then there appeared to them divided tongues, as of fire, and one sat upon each of them. And they were all filled with the Holy Spirit and began to speak with other tongues, as the Spirit gave them utterance." (Acts 2:1-4)

I'm not going to pretend that I understand what happened on the Day of Pentecost, but it is sufficient to say that fire was falling, and men were being consumed deep within with this holy fire.

This experience had never happened before, so those who obeyed the words of Jesus before ascending back to the Father were in for quite an experience with God.

God knew they needed this element, so He provided fire for this generation to advance His kingdom on earth. It wasn't by chance; it wasn't by mistake; it wasn't formulated in the mind of some theological genius; no sir, the fire came from heaven for such a time – and how we need this fire today!

Growing up in the faith through the Pentecostal movement, I regularly would hear the longing cry for God's Spirit to come and baptize us with holy fire. Calling the Lord for more extraordinary manifestations of power was customary. The call for deeper prayer life coupled with fasting was the order of the day. There seemed to be a deep yearning in the hearts of those gathered for God's touch.

No Substitutes!

As a young disciple of Christ, I quickly understood that this fire we all longed for was not on the For Sale table. It wasn't cheap! We must sacrifice and spend time with God to see His glory. The nature of God's glory was founded upon the premise that we had waited for Him, and finally, we were rewarded with His presence.

Those who were of like faith understood well that there were no substitutes for this glory. It would take a heart full of humility and brokenness if we were going to experience God at a whole new level. We all knew that, and those who wanted it would have to pay the high price of waiting in the secret place of prayer!

Suddenly!

On the day of Pentecost, the book of Acts says they were all in one accord, desiring the same thing – the promise of the Father. They were praying, seeking, and waiting for this promise Jesus told them about.

There was no timeline as to when God would answer, but they weren't keeping time, and they weren't keeping God in a box either. They just waited and waited and prayed and prayed until "**… suddenly, a sound from heaven, like a mighty rushing wind, filled the whole house where they were sitting. Then there appeared to them divided tongues, as of fire, and one sat upon each of them. And they were all filled with the Holy Spirit and began to speak with other tongues, as the Spirit gave them utterance.**" (Acts 2:1-4)

Suddenly, the yearning for a more profound experience with God was fulfilled. The Spirit of God fell upon each of them, and God's fire consumed those present. The supernatural experience of speaking in tongues accompanied this incredible experience, and God's seal was forever set upon His church.

Fire Without Paying the Cost!

I have been around many preachers and ministers around this country, and many talk about the fire of God. They talk about past experiences, past generations, etc., but only some acknowledge that they are without out. Many have lost the fire; all they have is a memory of what it once was!

I asked myself why there was no fire in the church. The answer is simple: There is no fire in the preachers! Why is there no fire in the preachers? There is no discipline to start a fire, much less keep one burning! The bottom line is that there is no genuine desire to pay the cost to see it happen. Let this sink in your heart.

As I bring this devotion to a close, I would like us to remember that a set of conditions usually precedes God's promises. These conditions must include obedience to the command, humility to be taught by God, perseverance to wait for what was promised, and faith to believe in the impossible.

I believe that without these elements activated in our lives, we will not experience a greater fullness of all that God has prepared for us. Neh'enah.

15

Who Is in Charge?

"And it came to pass, when Joshua was by Jericho, that he lifted his eyes and looked, and behold, a Man stood opposite him with His sword drawn in His hand. And Joshua went to Him and said to Him, "Are You for us or for our adversaries?" So He said, "No, but as Commander of the army of the LORD I have now come." And Joshua fell on his face to the earth and worshiped, and said to Him, "What does my Lord say to His servant?" Then the Commander of the LORD's army said to Joshua, "Take your sandal off your foot, for the place where you stand is holy." And Joshua did so." (Joshua 5:13-15)

As they entered the Promised Land, the beginning of a new chapter in the lives of the Hebrew children ensued, and now God was establishing a new order upon Joshua and His people.

After a long-awaited forty years in the wilderness, a new generation of warriors had risen to the occasion. God was about to teach this new generation, or as some call it, a Joshua Generation, to learn the heart of God.

If we read a little deeper into the leadership of Joshua, we will discover that this man was indeed a man of God who followed God wholeheartedly.

A few key things to note in these chapters in the book of Joshua is how the fear of God fell upon the Amorites and Canaanites. This generation of Hebrew children were brave men who feared God and wanted to please God.

When believers truly walk in the fear of the Lord and take godly action, even the world trembles at their commitment. The queen of Scotland used to say, *"I fear more the prayers of John Knox than an army of ten thousand men!"*

It was at this place called Gilgal that God took them to a different level of faith. This was also where the children of Israel, the new generation, got circumcised; yes, those were born in the wilderness, not the ones who came out of Egypt.

Also, allow me to mention that it was at this place where they kept the Passover and ate the produce of the land. Listen to this: **"And they ate of the produce of the land on the day after the Passover, unleavened bread and parched grain, on the very same day. Then the manna ceased on the day after they had eaten the produce of the land, and the children of Israel no longer had manna, but they ate the food of the land of Canaan that year."** (Joshua 5:11, 12)

As God's people began to exercise their faith, things began

to change for them, but not before. Too often, we are waiting for God to do something or everything for us; when He is waiting for us to act on what we know, the magic kicks in! This is divine order.

Same Wisdom - New Level!

It is easy to put our Christian life on cruise control and sit back and hope for the best, but let me tell you, our seeking after God must be intentional. We must always desire God to be first in all we do; His voice leads us and not our preferences or selfish plans. Let me emphasize that seeking after God's heart must be intentional!

I have often been challenged with why I keep pursuing God, 'Don't I know enough? Why not chill out and take it easy? After all, I have accomplished good things in the kingdom!'

No longer had I been bombarded with these thoughts that the Spirit of the Lord would raise a standard against those selfish thoughts! The race is not over until it's over!

A Fresh Encounter with God!

Why would anyone desire a new touch of God in their lives? After all, I'm saved; I read my Bible, pray daily, etc... Why fast? Why spend long nights in tears before God?

As Joshua was taking a deep breath and enjoying some of the victories under his belt in the Promised Land, something extraordinary took place…listen carefully to this:

"And it came to pass, when Joshua was by Jericho, that he lifted his eyes and looked, and behold, a Man stood opposite him with His sword drawn in His hand. And Joshua went to Him and said to Him, "Are You for us or for our adversaries?" So He said, "No, but as Commander of the army of the LORD I have now come." And Joshua fell on his face to the earth and worshiped, and said to Him, "What does my Lord say to His servant?" Then the Commander of the LORD's army said to Joshua, "Take your sandal off your foot, for the place where you stand is holy." And Joshua did so."

While near Jericho, Joshua lifted his eyes and saw a Man with a sword drawn in his hand. Joshua went to the Man and asked Him, **"Are You for us or for our adversaries?" The Man answered and said, "No, but as Commander of the army of the Lord I have come."**

Who was Joshua talking to? Who was this Man? It was Christ Jesus. It was Jesus in the Old Testament; these are called theophanies. [**Theophany:** Manifestation of God that is tangible to the human senses. In its most restrictive sense, it is a visible appearance of God in the Old Testament period often, but not always, in human form. Some would also include in this term Christophanies (preincarnate appearances of Christ) and angelophanies (appearances of angels)] - *Bakers Evangelical Dictionary of Biblical Theology*

As Joshua heard this Man speak, He knew who it was: God! He quickly **"fell on his face to the earth and worshiped, and said, "What does my Lord say to His servant?"**

The first thing when we truly see God, when we encounter a fresh revelation of Jesus, is to fall on our faces! A genuine encounter will bring us to a deeper place of worship. We are no longer willing to fight with God, give God ideas, or be in a bartering mode with God. At this point, all we want is to listen!

Take Off Your Sandals!

"Take your sandal off your foot, for the place where you stand is holy."

In ancient Bible times, taking off sandals always represented yielding your rights. The Man told him you are on holy ground and can't stand here with your choice request. It was God's way of saying to Joshua, "I have brought you this place, Joshua, and now I am about to lead you by the hand. You can't have anything else leading you or taking you. I must be All in All!

The Scripture goes on to say that Joshua did so.

In closing these thoughts, I have discovered that when God is ready to take you to another level, He will always call you to prayer and fasting, a new consecration of your life, and invite you to a selfless mindset. Are you ready for this? Neh'enah.

16

It's Getting Late: Knowing What Time It Is!

"And do this, knowing the time, that now it is high time to awake out of sleep; for now, our salvation is nearer than when we first believed. The night is far spent, the day is at hand. Therefore, let us cast off the works of darkness, and let us put on the armor of light. Let us walk properly, as in the day, not in revelry and drunkenness, not in lewdness and lust, not in strife and envy. But put on the Lord Jesus Christ, and make no provision for the flesh, to fulfill its lusts." (Romans 13:11-14)

The Apostle Paul felt the urgency to move with God's will during his day. It was apparent that this servant of the Lord lived with a burning zeal and longed to see the kingdom of God advance in the life of his followers and the primitive church.

Though Paul had already been involved in many church plantings and trained multiple servants for God's work, there was more to be done. He knew in himself that the Spirit of the Lord would testify of it to his inner man.

What Is High Time?

Informally, high time meant it was time to do something

that should have been done long ago! Also, in saying high time, we are saying that it should happen or be done now; it should have happened or been done sooner.

It was Paul's way of telling the church in Rome that we should have gotten our act together a long time ago!

In the revelation God has been speaking to me about, I want to deal with a few things that the Holy Spirit wants to bring to the forefront today regarding high time.

I believe that too many times, we don't like God to tell us what to do or when to do it, yet we allow the flesh countless times to lead us astray one and time again. Let your mind dwell on this.

Joshua's Challenge!

First, let us look at Joshua as he prepared to lead God's people into the promised land. Listen to the word of God: **"After the death of Moses the servant of the LORD, it came to pass that the LORD spoke to Joshua the son of Nun, Moses' assistant, saying: "Moses My servant is dead. Now therefore, arise, go over this Jordan, you and all these people, to the land which I am giving to them— the children of Israel."** (Joshua 1:1, 2)

I want to turn your attention and focus on the countless times we have waited upon the Lord, all with good intentions, for direction. Should we go? Should we stop? Should we turn? Should we jump in? Etc.

Many questions are legit, and perhaps the circumstances don't look favorable to the human eye, but then again, God doesn't need our approval to do His work His way! Too often, we have lingered behind and stayed back due to fear and uncertainty.

Jesus said, "It's Getting Late!"

In another story in the book of John, chapter 9:1-5, Jesus spoke to His disciples of time. In not too many words, Jesus, in essence, said, I only have a short time, then the opportunity will cease!

You and I have but a short time in this life. We must get to the place where God needs us to be. You must know whether in business or ministry or be positioned in a more excellent way to walk with God. We can't wonder what is happening in our world or blame politicians, the economy, the government, or the church for every mishap. Sooner or later, we must take responsibility for why our lives are not where God needs them to be!

Listen to what Jesus said, **"Now as Jesus passed by, He saw a man who was blind from birth. And His disciples asked Him, saying, "Rabbi, who sinned, this man or his parents, that he was born blind?" Jesus answered,**

"Neither this man nor his parents sinned, but that the works of God should be revealed in him. I must work the works of Him who sent Me while it is day; the night is coming when no one can work. As long as I am in the world, I am the light of the world."

Hear and obey!

As I get ready to close this devotion, let me say that unless a man or woman of God has a relationship with the living God and a willingness to be alone with God as to be taught by God, that man or that woman will only gain a reputation as "saved" or "Christians," but no more!

The faithful servant of Jesus must be willing to pray until God's desires and zeal impregnate them. Once empowered by God's Spirit, that servant of God must trust and obey all that God told him to do. We go in faith or fear for the rest of our lives! Neh'enah.

… Volume 8

17

The Time is Now!

"But as He went, the multitudes thronged Him. Now a woman, having a flow of blood for twelve years, who had spent all her livelihood on physicians and could not be healed by any, came from behind and touched the border of His garment. And immediately, her flow of blood stopped. And Jesus said, "Who touched Me?" When all denied it, Peter, and those with him said, "Master, the multitudes throng and press You, and You say, 'Who touched Me?'" But Jesus said, "Somebody touched Me, for I perceived power going out from Me." Now when the woman saw that she was not hidden, she came trembling and falling before Him; she declared to Him in the presence of all the people the reason she had touched Him and how she was healed immediately. And He said to her, "Daughter, be of good cheer; your faith has made you well. Go in peace." (Luke 8:42-48)

As we read these passages, you will recognize this familiar story - the woman who had a blood issue for 12 years. This woman had been in bondage to this physical illness for a long time and was now desperate. Have you ever been in an area of despair yourself? It is not a place of joy and exuberant happiness!

Called to be Normal.

If we look back a bit into the woman's life, according to what the Scripture says about her, we can make some assumptions about what may have taken place in it. Again, we don't know everything, but it is enough to make some practical applications to our lives.

Open your imagination and let us dive in and study this woman who was trapped inside her illness for 12 years.

The Scripture begins by saying that **"a woman, having a flow of blood for twelve years, who had spent all her livelihood on physicians and could not be healed by any…."**

If you care to imagine with me, you can already guess that this woman had been experiencing an issue of blood or menstrual cycle that wouldn't stop. It was ongoing and perhaps embarrassing to share with anyone; I don't believe she went around asking her friends or telling her friends about her situation, at least not at first.

As the flow continued, things were not to be taken lightly any longer. It was becoming more severe by the day. She finally decides to visit the doctor, but no one can give her an answer to her issue, much less provide any healing for her. From one doctor, she goes to another and another and another. Money is now an issue as she can't afford to pay, not to mention she was not getting better. Can you imagne the desperation? Can you picture the oppression and depression that kept her up night after night?

Out of Line?

If there is something I know about myself, it is that when my life is out of line, I cannot rest. I can't find peace; I can't find joy; I can't find a purpose for existing. My life goes in circles because I must find the remedy for my emotional duress.

Can you imagine the trap? Unable to talk to anyone about her problem, unable to attend the synagogue for a weekly gathering, unable to have family over, unable to fulfill her role as a woman, imagine it. She was conquered by fear, doubt, and unbelief!

I am meeting more and more believers who love the Lord. Still, they are trapped by lies, insecurities, and fear, enslaved to people's opinions, which renders them ineffective and unproductive.

Living this way may become a challenge at first, but then one succumbs to the more potent force and finally conforms to this mold for many years. This lifestyle then becomes your identity. Everyone will know you by your struggle, not your knowledge of Christ!

The Scripture also tells us that the woman had to visit many doctors, but none could help her. This tells us that the Spirit of God has often awakened us to move in faith and trust God, but we didn't! We don't! We stay married to the idea that "this is how life is for me!" This is a lie from the very pit of hell!

Coming from Behind!

"...came from behind and touched the border of His garment. And immediately her flow of blood stopped. And Jesus said, "Who touched Me?" When all denied it, Peter and those with him said, "Master, the multitudes throng and press You, and You say, 'Who touched Me?' "But Jesus said, "Somebody touched Me, for I perceived power going out from Me."

When did this woman get the courage, strength, or faith to make this move? The point here is that she made it! She wasn't going to live this type of life one more day! She was sick to the core; she was poor and ostracized by family and friends. Something had to change, and the time was now!

Everyone around Jesus wanted something from him but never got what they came for because they needed faith. Listen to this, **"But let him ask in faith, with no doubting, for he who doubts is like a wave of the sea driven and tossed by the wind. For let not that man suppose**

that he will receive anything from the Lord; he is a double-minded man, unstable in all his ways." (James 1:6-8)

Who Touched Me?

"But Jesus said, "Somebody touched Me, for I perceived power going out from Me."

Here is Jesus Himself testifying about what happens when He is touched by someone with faith, God's faith. **Jesus said, "I perceived power going out from Me."**

As I close this devotion, please understand one thing: Unless we respond to an awakened spirit of faith in us and obey it, we will never see the changes God wants from us. We can't change in our power; we can't be followers of Christ in our power or change our lives just because we feel good and ready, no sir. Unless the spirit of God draws us, we cannot come!

We will always know when it's our time to follow Him! Neh'enah.

18

Rewired by God!

"But seek first the kingdom of God and His righteousness, and all these things shall be added to you." (Matthew 6:33)

While in prayer and fasting this morning, I was in the Spirit, and God gave me a vision. Allow me to share this beautiful insight into God's heart:

As I was praying at our ministry base early in the morning, the Spirit of God gave me a vision of an electrician who had some wire cutters and was cutting about four electrical wires. At this point, I asked the Lord, what is this man doing? The Lord told me, David, this man is cutting some cables in the wrong place. They have been wired wrong. So, he is fixing the root cause of the problem and why there is no electricity. I must admit that I was puzzled and so proceeded to inquire of the Lord what the whole dream meant and what it had to do with my life or anyone's life—the end of the dream.

The Lord caused my heart to gain understanding and wisdom by telling me that our lives are wired, but they are wrong. Our lives are wired to work in the realm of the natural, the commonsense type of way. The Lord told me things don't work for people because they operate without proper grounding. They are only running with limited strength and power. That is why people worry, become anxious, and become overly concerned about life.

When the Lord Jesus is invited into the human heart and invited to live there and make His home there, that person becomes a new creation according to 1 Corinthians 5:17.

In this latest creation; it must be wired differently than in the natural. Many of our previous life habits must be rewired. Our thinking, our philosophy of life, our ideas of how things should be or not be, our process patterns, and so forth… God must rewire all these.

The rewiring must be done according to God's standards and in a way that gives Christ preeminence and places Him as the highest priority in our lives. This would be a thorough rewiring!

Living in Cruise Control!

The rewiring of God has to do with alignment with His will. Too often, many so-called believers live their lives on cruise control. They don't have daily encounters with the Spirit of God or His word. They are living on yesterday's manna, on yesterday's experience. There is no renewal of His presence in their lives, and they have become stagnant.

I'm not saying they are bad parents, employees, or valuable to society. They are probably precious to many people on a social level but have never become useful to God. The Lord probably doesn't personally know them!

I am talking to you about individuals who have not allowed God to fully take over their lives. Consequently, they live lives full of worry and anxiety and are burdened by everything that surrounds them. This, in turn, has affected them in terms of experiencing peace, joy, and even love, not to mention the countless disappointments of daily living.

Allow God to Rewire Your Life!

Here are a few notes on how to allow God to rewire our lives.

    1. First, we must understand the words of Jesus when He said, "But seek first the kingdom of God and His righteousness, and all these things shall be added to you." As we live our lives under the guidance of His Holy Spirit, He will always lead us by divine order. Everything the Spirit of God does has to do with the correct wiring. He will never wire us any different than how God wants it done!

I venture to say that most, if not all, of our issues stem from an unwillingness to be wired by the Spirit of God.

We are unwilling to yield, surrender, or allow the Lord to show us His way! Because of this form of living, we are stuck with fleshly ideas (wrong wiring), and corruption is our reward.

2. Secondly, we should ask God to give us discernment so that we will know what to do in any situation. We must learn the discipline of filtering all our thoughts through the Holy Spirit before we allow ourselves to feel and act.

Once we know that the thoughts that we are having are not from the Spirit of God or His Word, then we must conclude that these thoughts are not God's will for us. We must take these thoughts captive first and foremost to the obedience of Christ.

"We are destroying sophisticated arguments and every exalted and proud thing that sets itself up against the [true] knowledge of God, and we are taking every thought and purpose captive to the obedience of Christ..." (2 Corinthians 10:5)

The sooner we can quiet these wicked and selfish thoughts of fear and insecurity, the quicker we can allow the Spirit of God to minister to us. If we don't take these thoughts down by Christ's authority, we will fall prey to them and be overcome with anxiety, fear, doubt, and countless negative emotions.

3. Finally, the words in Colossians 3:1-3 must be applied once and daily during our Christian journey. This is what it says, **"Therefore if you have been raised with Christ** [to a new life, sharing in His resurrection from the dead], **keep seeking the things that are above, where Christ is, seated at the right hand of God. Set your mind and keep focused habitually on the things above** [the heavenly things], **not on things that are on the earth** [which have only temporal value]. **For you died** [to this world], **and your** [new, real] **life is hidden with Christ in God. When Christ, who is our life, appears, then you also will appear with Him in glory."** (Colossians 3:1-4)

Seeking those things above is challenging. It takes discipline! With discipline, you can focus on what is needed to walk in victory daily. As one of my mentors said, we must always fight for the right way to live!

The temptation to keep living in the natural (wired wrong) is always present. The flesh only knows to sin and live a defeated life; we must discipline ourselves to seek the things above, where Christ is. This, too, is also part of the rewiring of God! Neh'enah.

19

The Harvest is Ready!

"Jesus said to them, "My food is to do the will of Him who sent Me, and to finish His work. Do you not say, 'There are still four months and then comes the harvest'? Behold, I say to you, lift up your eyes and look at the fields, for they are already white for harvest!" (John 4:34-35)

"After these things the Lord appointed seventy others also, and sent them two by two before His face into every city and place where He Himself was about to go. Then He said to them, "The harvest truly is great, but the laborers are few; therefore pray the Lord of the harvest to send out laborers into His harvest. Go your way; behold, I send you out as lambs among wolves. Carry neither money bag, knapsack, nor sandals; and greet no one along the road. But whatever house you enter, first say, 'Peace to this house.'" (Luke 10:1-5)

In my meditations this week, I came across some compelling words given by the Master. These were not just words uttered to educate me but delivered with much passion straight from the heart of God. God shared His heart with me as I pondered His deep zeal for the lost.

Are There Still Four Months?

In our pursuit to follow the heart of God, the command has been given. In Mark 16:15, Jesus said, **"Go into all the world and preach the gospel to every creature."** We don't need someone to define this for us. It is laid out in red letters. Jesus said, "Go!"

In my seeking after God's heart, I have experienced much when it comes to testifying to the lost regarding the mercy and compassion of God. Some thank me, others criticize, and others are not interested in the gospel of the kingdom.

When Jesus sent His disciples, He didn't tell them to analyze what they thought of them or, if they criticized them, turn around and go home and cry! No, He said, "Keep going."

Don't let anyone discourage you from witnessing or from declaring the goodness and mercy of God to them. God's eternal plan is second to none; lost sinners don't know it! Jesus commands us to "Go!"

Listen to the counsel of God when it comes to sharing the bread of God with the world:
**"Cast your bread upon the waters,
For you will find it after many days.
Give a serving to seven, and also to eight,
For you do not know what evil will be on the earth.**

If the clouds are full of rain,
They empty themselves upon the earth;
And if a tree falls to the south or the north,
In the place where the tree falls, there it shall lie.
He who observes the wind will not sow,
And he who regards the clouds will not reap.
As you do not know what is the way of the wind,
Or how the bones grow in the womb of her who is with child,
So you do not know the works of God who makes everything.
In the morning, sow your seed,
And in the evening, do not withhold your hand;
For you do not know which will prosper,
Either this or that,
Or whether both alike will be good." (Ecclesiastes 11:1-6)

One of the highest responsibilities for all believers when walking with God is sharing the word with those who don't know Christ intimately. Don't let anyone stop you or convince you not to do it!

Jesus Appoints Seventy to Go!

In Luke 10, Jesus appoints seventy servants to take the gospel of the kingdom to cities that Jesus had planned on going to.

Here's what Jesus reveals:

"The harvest truly is great, but the laborers are few; therefore pray the Lord of the harvest to send out laborers into His harvest."

1) First, Jesus reveals that the harvest is plentiful! Can you imagine it now if it was great in great quantity? There are lost people who don't intimately know Jesus. Family, friends, backsliders, etc., don't know Him, and we must tell them.

2) Secondly, Jesus makes it a point to say that the laborers are few. This goes without saying, but it is true. People want to sit and hear and learn the word, which is all good—but the need to speak for Jesus has never been greater. Now, I know that not everyone has the boldness or the evangelist anointing, but we have all been called to speak for God and to testify of His mercy.

3) Thirdly, Jesus told us to pray to the Lord of the harvest to send laborers into His harvest. God is calling us to intercede so that people will be open to hearing and receiving the gospel and so that God can raise other workers to impact Jesus in their world.

4) Lastly, listen to this: **"Go your way; behold, I send you out as lambs among wolves."** As Jesus brings this challenge to a close, He says something that will forever be embedded in our hearts - He said you are going as lambs among wolves. In other words, it will not be easy

telling others about Jesus! We are dealing with "wolves!" Jesus said it. Expect rejection, criticism, and even some beatings for the sake of Christ.

As I close, I'm reminded of this old hymn that touched my life very early on as I surrendered to serve Jesus with all that I had:

Hear The Lord Of Harvest Sweetly Calling.
"Who Will Go And Work For Me Today?
Who Will Bring To Me The Lost And Dying?
Who Will Point Them To The Narrow Way?"

Speak, My Lord, Speak My Lord,
Speak, And I'll Be Quick To Answer Thee;
Speak, My Lord, Speak, My Lord,
Speak, And I Will Answer, "Lord, Send Me."
When The Coal Of Fire Touched The Prophet,
Making Him As Pure As Pure Can Be.
When The Voice Of God, Said "Who'll Go For Us?"
The He Answered, "Here I Am , Send Me."
Millions Now In Sin And Shame Are Dying;
Listen To Their Sad And Bitter Cry;
Hasten, Brother, Hasten To The Rescue;
Quickly Answer, "Master, Here Am I."
Soon The Time For Reaping Will Be Over;
Soon We'll Gather For The Harvest Home;
May The Lord Of Harvest Smile Upon Us,
May We Hear His Blessed, "Child, Well Done."

George Bennard (1873-1958) was born in Youngstown, OH. When he was a child, the family moved to Albia, Iowa. He served with the Salvation Army in Iowa for several years before he was ordained in the Methodist Episcopal Church. Neh'enah.

20

Trained in Character by Obstacles!

"Now these are the nations which the LORD left, that He might test Israel by them, that is, all who had not known any of the wars in Canaan (this was only so that the generations of the children of Israel might be taught to know war, at least those who had not formerly known it), namely, five lords of the Philistines, all the Canaanites, the Sidonians, and the Hivites who dwelt in Mount Lebanon, from Mount Baal Hermon to the entrance of Hamath. And they were left, that He might test Israel by them, to know whether they would obey the commandments of the LORD, which He had commanded their fathers by the hand of Moses." (Judges 3:1-4)

As you read the text above, can you believe what God did in this portion of Scripture? Can you see how the wisdom of God operates with His people? Can you see it happening in your own life?

God left the pagan tribes so that He would test the younger Hebrew children to war through them. No wonder God leaves difficult people in our lives; no wonder God allows difficulty around us occasionally; no wonder things can go so smoothly in one season only to experience chaos in the next!

In the book of Judges, the Scripture says that God didn't remove the pagan tribes from their midst because He had another thing in mind; God wanted to use those pagan tribes in Canaan to test His people, Israel! How about that?

Too many times, believers wonder why God allows negative things to continue existing in their lives. They see life's obstacles as hindrances to their advancement and feel that if it weren't for those negative things, their lives would be so much better.

How many times have you thought this very thought? "My life would be so much better, or I would be so far ahead if it weren't for this situation!" I do believe we are all guilty that, at some point, we all complained or whined before God about our lot in life.

Well, the time has come for us to know God's intent on obstacles and adversity in our lives.

God Uses Pagan Nations to Train His People for Personal War!

If there is something God is consistent in doing with us who believe, it is to train us for war by using pagan tribes, worldly people, or daily secular situations. Yes, God will use all these to equip the saints for the work of the ministry and to mature them in manners concerning the advancement of the gospel on earth.

I know that believers have been taught many things in their walk with God: some of it is based on false doctrine; others are taught with an imbalanced view of God's heart; yet others are trained with extreme viewpoints of the Christian faith.

Just because life is not rainbows and sunshine for you, it doesn't mean God is not King over the universe! It is not always the devil's fault that you can't balance your checkbook, your tires are flat, or your car won't start. God knows you need to purchase new equipment for your car; perhaps take an introductory course on budgeting your finances, etc.

I am saying that life happens to all—sinners and saved ones alike! Those who understand God's work in the believer's heart, mind, and character will always reap the most significant portion. These are the ones who end up in leadership positions in both ministry and secular positions.

God Is After Character Development!

If we are not careful, we will think that everything is spiritually directed and exclude ourselves from the equation of ever making decisions that affect our present day. We will neglect the responsibility of caring for what God has given us to do and shift to blaming spiritual forces for our laziness, lack of discipline, and negligence!

God left pagan tribes so Israel could learn to fight! They would be tested repeatedly for the simple reason that God needed to know their hearts, **"And they were left, that He might test Israel by them, to know whether they would obey the commandments of the LORD ..."**.

Nations, people, obstacles, etc. that appear outwardly mighty don't scare God; they don't scare me; do they scare you? The only reason God allows adversity in your life and mine is so that He knows if we will stay in His character and have the courage to keep His commandments or turn our backs on His commandments when the going gets tough!

Always remember: Adversity in our midst has many purposes, but the main one is to see if you have the courage to stay with God or not! Neh'enah.

21

Why Is This Happening to Me?

"Then the children of Israel did evil in the sight of the LORD. So the LORD delivered them into the hand of Midian for seven years, and the hand of Midian prevailed against Israel." (Judges 6:1, 2)

"Now the Angel of the LORD came and sat under the terebinth tree which was in Ophrah, which belonged to Joash the Abiezrite, while his son Gideon threshed wheat in the winepress, in order to hide it from the Midianites. And the Angel of the LORD appeared to him, and said to him, "The LORD is with you, you mighty man of valor!" Gideon said to Him, "O my lord, if the LORD is with us, why then has all this happened to us? And where are all His miracles which our fathers told us about, saying, 'Did not the LORD bring us up from Egypt?' But now the LORD has forsaken us and delivered us into the hands of the Midianites." (Judges 6:11-13)

Here is a lesson for the ages....

One of the questions that stood out to me as I meditated this day on this portion of Scripture is when Gideon asked the Angel of the Lord, **"O my lord, if the Lord is with us,**

why then has all this happened to us?"

I want to bring this one thought to the forefront: often, we, as a people, tend to get so caught up in our own lives that we forsake the will of the Father or change our priorities from putting God at the very top of the list to making Him second, third, or last!

As much as we don't want to admit the fact, I know we have all done it, consciously or unconsciously.

Interrupted!

First, we must make note that interruptions do happen in our lives. Things can be going well, and then, without warning, the bottom falls off! You have been there!

We can have glorious breakthroughs and what we would call bright days when we suddenly get that phone call, a text, or an email that changes everything that matters to us. Yes, we are left in a tailspin, wondering what happened. I know you know what I am talking about.

The interruption would be the first mysterious occurrence, but like it, the next question, "OK. But why?" So, we find ourselves questioning this random interruption and then the why. Please note that this is not unusual for God to do in our lives.

Not Aligned!

Judges 6:1 and 2 reveal the mystery: **"Then the children of Israel did evil in the sight of the LORD. So, the LORD delivered them into the hand of Midian for seven years, and the hand of Midian prevailed against Israel."**

When Israel did evil in the sight of the Lord, the favor of God seemed to cease! Do you see it? Everything was flowing very well until Israel decided to make some moves independently. They got too confident and probably forsook the Lord's grace and covering.

Anytime we step out of bounce with God, we can count on the Lord bringing some personal judgment on us. He will stop important things because He knows we will stop and listen to counsel.

At this point, the Angel of the Lord came to visit Gideon while he threshed wheat at the winepress in hiding from the Midianites. The fact that Gideon is hiding doesn't sound like Israel is walking in favor of God. Something has transpired, and Israel's confidence in Almighty God is at an all-time low; they are not courageous and bold like lions but somewhat afraid of the enemy and hiding from them.

Sin and compromise had moved in, and Israel had abandoned the Lord's provision. They were now slaves to fear because of their evil heart against Jehovah God.

We can only do that for some time until God shows up to vindicate His holy name before the wicked.

Lord, but why?

"O my lord, if the LORD is with us, why then has all this happened to us? "

Gideon was not ignorant of Israel's faults and sins. He knew exactly what Israel was into and doing at the time. He knew that God was not happy with them…so why ask the question, why then has all this happened to us?

Too often, modern believers think they can live in outright sin and still be blessed by God. They feel that since God is not bringing any discipline to them, it's okay to keep practicing all kinds of transgressions and iniquities.

I don't think Gideon was excusing Israel's sin, but he probably thought God was powerful and that if He took us out of Egypt once, He could do it again. All this is true, but not without repentance or spiritual reformation!

We can learn from this: If God allows an interruption in your life, wisdom will say, "You should find out why the interruption." It might be that we are out of alignment with His will. There might be some hindrance in our character that we need to attend to, such as holding the flow of God in our life, family, business, ministry, etc. Neh'enah.

22

Abide at All Costs!

"I am the true vine, and My Father is the vinedresser. Every branch in Me that does not bear fruit He takes away; and every branch that bears fruit He prunes, that it may bear more fruit. You are already clean because of the word which I have spoken to you. Abide in Me, and I in you. As the branch cannot bear fruit of itself unless it abides in the vine, neither can you, unless you abide in Me. "I am the vine; you are the branches. He who abides in Me, and I in him, bears much fruit; for without Me, you can do nothing. If anyone does not abide in Me, he is cast out as a branch and is withered; and they gather them and throw them into the fire, and they are burned. If you abide in Me, and My words abide in you, you will ask what you desire, and it shall be done for you. By this My Father is glorified, that you bear much fruit; so, you will be My disciples." (John 15:1-8)

In my devotion today, I came across one of the most potent life principles Jesus laid out—the principle of abiding in Him.

Before I share insight into this powerful life principle, let me say how drastically our world has changed in the last twenty years. Not only has the secular world gone off the cliff, but the church has also turned the true gospel of Christ into a nice, powerless story and our corporate settings into social gatherings—and people love it so!

The church has chosen a path that promotes religion without power, a gospel story that speaks only of how to get blessed, and is caught up in this selfish cycle of "help me God, cause I'm suffering!" If you look closely, it is usually the same people that come for prayer. The same individuals are constantly struggling with the same old thing!

It is no different in the secular realm: The same people are always at the doctor's clinic, the same people who borrow money at the finance company, and the same people who are always getting counseling for this or that. Have you noticed this?

Yes, but why?

In the secular realm, people are unwilling to make any changes that will improve their lives relationally, financially, physically, and emotionally. They won't do it!

It's too expensive, requires too much sacrifice, and requires too much discipline to make it work. You and I have been here countless times.

Guess what? The church is in the same predicament. Same problems; different side of the spectrum. Unbelievers don't know the power of God but won't even trust in psychology, medicine, counseling, etc. They have no discipline to make a better life for themselves, even if their life depended on it.

Now, believers know the power of God but won't allow themselves to be led by it.

The Vinedresser

Jesus said He was the true Vine, and the Father was the farmer, the vinedresser. It was in the farmer's judgment to see which branch needed to be taken off and which branch needed to be pruned so that it may produce more fruit.

The vinedresser knew with precision what branch needed some work. All this could only happen based on the specific branch connected to the Vine. If it was connected, that branch had a future in producing fruit. If the branch had been broken off, perhaps by strong winds (trials, etc.), it would have to be taken away and thrown into the fire.

Abide in Me and I in You!

As Jesus speaks, He makes a powerful statement that shakes the core of everyone listening to Him. He said, **"Abide in Me, and I in you. As the branch cannot bear fruit of itself unless it abides in the vine, neither can you unless you abide in Me."**

Jesus said that fruit could not come forth of itself! The life that Jesus gives through this abiding is unique. It's His very life!

Life always produces after its kind. The life of God produces the things of God; fleshly natural life produces fleshly things. Spiritual people look for spiritual things; carnal people look for carnal things.

What Does Abide Mean?

The word abide means different things, but it is about staying connected. Let us look at some of these:

1. To remain in a place.
2. To tarry.
3. To stay in the house.
4. To stay overnight.
5. To dwell.
6. To stay alive.
7. To remain in a sphere.
8. To stand against opposition.
9. To hold out.
10. To stand fast.
11. To remain in legal force.
12. To remain, to stay still, opp. To move, to be moved, to
]   be changed. (self)
13. To remain undisturbed.
14. To wait.

Jesus continued reiterating this principle: **"I am the vine; you are the branches. He who abides in Me, and I in him, bears much fruit; for without Me you can do nothing."**

In essence, Jesus is saying to those of us who believe that if we abide in Him, we will produce much fruit. Fruit is the expression of someone or something that has been embedded in life.

Obstacles to Abiding!

We have already heard what Jesus said about abiding. We have learned the reasons why we should continue to stay in Him. Jesus said that without Him, we can't do anything!

So, what obstacles continually move us away from Christ and take us away from abiding in His presence?

Here is a short list of what has been the stumbling block to many servants, and most of these have to do with an undisciplined mindset.

    1. **"Now the ones that fell among thorns are those who, when they have heard, go out and are choked with cares, riches, and pleasures of life, and bring no fruit to maturity."** (Luke 8:14)

Nothing hinders our spiritual growth like giving ourselves

over to the undisciplined mindset of worrying about the things of this life, such as care, riches, and pleasures.

Please know I'm not promoting carelessness with family, finances, or vacation time. This is not what this Scripture is referring to. It refers to believers who are wishy-washy in their minds and their thinking. They pursue everything that has nothing to do with God all the time. It is the story of their lives!

    2. **"You, therefore, must endure hardship as a good soldier of Jesus Christ. No one engaged in warfare entangles himself with the affairs of this life that he may please him who enlisted him as a soldier."** (2 Timothy 2:3, 4)

One of the most incredible things I see lacking in God's people today is discipline. Believers live such undisciplined lives that it is no wonder they are constantly struggling with stuff. By stuff, I mean sin, health, finances, and relationships, which affect their lives in all areas.

The Apostle Paul calls the young disciple Timothy to attention and says, **"You must endure hardship as a good soldier of Jesus Christ. No one engaged in warfare entangles himself with the affairs of this life that he may please him who enlisted him as a soldier."**

The word engaged in warfare means that you are already

part of an army at war. He says that the soldier doesn't entangle [to weave in, to entwine, i.e., to involve with] with the affairs of life. You must take care of life, but don't become entwined with it so that you may please him who enlisted you as a soldier, Christ!

3. Stay abiding in Him because our future depends on it. Too often, we think of the future and what it will bring. How do we make our lives better and bring about a better future? People have so much fear regarding their future that they can't function well now.

Often, we think that our future depends upon someone else making it happen or the right opportunity coming our way. We might be waiting for the stars to line up or the moon to be turned to blood, but...

Let me tell you something I have learned in my walk with God as I make every effort to abide in Him - I have learned this one secret: My future is not somewhere in the distance; the future is found in me. The future is in the seed. As I abide in Him, my future is being written and manifested.

You see, the future of a forest is found in its seed. As the seed abides in the ground, its future (a tree) will come. It is the same with you and me.

My future is set if I cultivate my life by abiding in Him. I will bear fruit in this life; God's wishes will be fulfilled, and God's will be done in me and through me. Neh'enah.

23

Stirred!

"So, the woman bore a son and called his name Samson, and the child grew, and the LORD blessed him. And the Spirit of the LORD began to move upon him at Mahaneh Dan between Zorah and Eshtaol." (Judges 13:24, 25)

When I think of this specific story of how Samson's mother was barren and how God brought her a son, it is beyond me how and why God would do that. I don't think Samson's mother was the only barren woman in Zorah. There had to be others, I'm sure.

All I can think of is that when God has something in His mind and His heart to do, He will bypass or defy common knowledge; He will surpass our understanding and proceed to prove Himself as the Great I AM. You see, only our heavenly Father can do this.

Chosen Out of Barrenness!

Now, why would God choose this woman? Why would God insist on selecting a barren woman? He could have chosen a woman who could bear children or was fertile enough to bring a son or daughter to Manoah. Why go the long way? Why go the impossible route? Why defy science? I don't know, but God did!

In God's wisdom, the Lord always looks for an opportunity to demonstrate His power and glory! The Lord loves to show His nature during impossibilities—amen. Nothing is impossible for the Lord; Scripture lets us know.

Our natural eye sees barrenness; fruitfulness is what the Lord has created before the world's foundations! **"...for he who comes to God must believe that He is and that He is a rewarder of those who diligently seek Him."** (Hebrews 11:6)

Chosen!

Before Samson was born, the Lord had already commissioned the parents to offer their son back to him and for them to keep Samson under a Nazarite vow. God had plans for this baby birthed out of barrenness. No one would be taking credit for Samson's victories and demonstrations of power. Only God!

God again shows us that He doesn't need any help regarding skill, ability, and unique gifting to get His will done on earth. He will use what He raises! If God has raised you, it is sufficient to say that all God needs is your obedience!

It is also evident that God was unto something with this young Samson. The Scripture says that the child grew, and the Lord blessed him. This was for all those around him to see as a testimony of God's faithfulness. This is external.

Now, let us look at the internal work of God. The Scripture further says, **"And the Spirit of the Lord began to move upon him..."**. The Lord was blessing him not only outwardly but internally as well. God had possessed this man with holy fire.

You see, it is one thing to know the favor of God externally, and this is all well and good, but the inward part, where God lives and dwells in us, is the true mark of spiritual growth. People are enamored with the externals, almost as if they need an affirmation that God is moving and doing things. If God moves by His Spirit deep within, anything external is just the icing on the cake!

The Scripture says, **"...the Spirit of the Lord began to move upon him (Samson)..."**. The word move means to thrust, to compel, to stir.

We must pursue this enduement of power for our lives. Our future as believers depends upon it!

Unless we recognize the Spirit's movement in our lives, we will be ineffective in our testimony for Jesus. Our witness will need more convincing power, and our lifestyle will give us away as nominal casual Christians! Unless the

Spirit of the Lord moves upon and within us, we will lack the presence that makes us distinctive from the world or the carnal church.

Time to Wait Until ...

"Behold, I send the Promise of My Father upon you; but tarry in the city of Jerusalem until you are endued with power from on high." (Luke 24:49)

If there is any formula to the resident manifest power of God in us, it is the act of waiting for it or Him. Wait upon the Lord in prayer and fasting until the fire descends upon you. God is faithful and will fill us if we are trustworthy, honest, and desperate enough. I have seen it in my own life, and I have seen it in the lives of others. If we wait, we will receive power from on high!

Here's the promise:
"But you shall receive power when the Holy Spirit has come upon you; and you shall be witnesses to Me in Jerusalem, and in all Judea and Samaria, and to the end of the earth." (Acts 1:8) Neh'enah.

24

When Jesus Says, "I Don't Know You!"

"And He went through the cities and villages, teaching, and journeying toward Jerusalem. Then one said to Him, "Lord, are there few who are saved?" And He said to them, "Strive to enter through the narrow gate, for many, I say to you, will seek to enter and will not be able. When once the Master of the house has risen up and shut the door, and you begin to stand outside and knock at the door, saying, 'Lord, Lord, open for us,' and He will answer and say to you, 'I do not know you, where you are from,' then you will begin to say, 'We ate and drank in Your presence, and You taught in our streets.' But He will say, 'I tell you I do not know you, where you are from. Depart from Me, all you workers of iniquity.' There will be weeping and gnashing of teeth, when you see Abraham and Isaac and Jacob and all the prophets in the kingdom of God, and yourselves thrust out. They will come from the east and the west, from the north and the south, and sit down in the kingdom of God. And indeed, there are last who will be first, and there are first who will be last." (Luke 13:22-30)

Recently, while in prayer and meditation, the Spirit of the Lord caused my heart and mind to focus on this one passage of Scripture about intimacy with God and what it means to be in union with Christ.

I know that people like to voice their opinions on what it means to be a Christian and what constitutes being a servant of God.

When it comes to the Christian religion, many people say that they are Christian because they aren't or form part of the Roman Catholic, Mormon, or Jehovah's Witness church. They might even say they don't believe in worshipping saints, candles, or idols. That is all good, but that doesn't make you a believer.

According to the Scriptures, a believer has experienced God's inward life through the Holy Spirit, better known as being born-again by the Spirit of God. The Spirit of the Lord will enter a man's heart and mind and begin to lead them in the ways of God.

As a born-again believer, one begins to grow in God's knowledge by reading the Scriptures and spending time in personal prayer and devotion. The deeper one enters this mindset, the greater the knowledge of God.

Spending time in prayer and God's Word until a fresh revelation of God comes out of the experience is called having intimacy with God. The believer can now walk in a new level of intimacy with God by obeying the Word of God and the prophetic revelation imparted by the Spirit of God.

Therefore, the born-again experience is not an outward experience but an inward experience.

Let us move on to our story, as it begins in Luke 13:22.

It Sounds Like the Training of an Army!

"And He went through the cities and villages, teaching, and journeying toward Jerusalem. Then one said to Him, "Lord, are there few who are saved?" (Luke 13:22)

At this time, Christ was preaching and teaching in the villages when someone asked, **"Lord, are there few who are saved?"**

People ask many questions, but occasionally, you get people who ask life-changing questions like this.

Jesus responded: **"Strive to enter through the narrow gate, for many, I say to you, will seek to enter and will not be able."**

Jesus said that when the opportunity comes your way to enter the kingdom, take the opportunity. God does not always give us a chance to enter His kingdom. Jesus didn't say it would be easy; Jesus said it would be a fight to join. He said, **"Strive to enter through the narrow gate."**

In other words, one must be desperate to enter; otherwise, he will not. This doesn't sound like a religion for the weak-hearted or the undisciplined. It sounds more to me like the building or training of an army.

Time Is Running Out!

In every generation since the Christian church has been around, there have been many impactful moments where the gospel of the kingdom advanced forcefully.

There have also been times when the church of Jesus was persecuted for its advancement. Every person who made Jesus the Lord of their lives understands that they belong to the army of God and that walking with God is not a game, a social club, or a place to show off your status as a citizen. Being in Christ means that you are a soldier and are under marching orders every day of your life!

Now, Jesus continued his discourse and added this to the previous question: **"When once the Master of the house has risen up and shut the door, and you begin to stand outside and knock at the door, saying, 'Lord, Lord, open for us,'..."**

Jesus was telling the servant that there was a time coming when the Master would rise and shut the door and that, at that time, it would be too late to get in. No one would be able to enter the kingdom. Imagine this!

What About Those Outside?

"...and you begin to stand outside and knock at the door, saying, 'Lord, Lord, open for us,' and He will answer and say to you, 'I do not know you, where you are from'..."

The inevitable happened; people stayed outside because the time for the door to close had come!

Those who were left outside began to plead for a second chance. As the knocking persisted, a voice came from inside, saying, **"I don't know you!"** The Master could hear the knock, but He didn't know who these people were; therefore, He wasn't opening the door for them.

Once that plea didn't work, they made a more vigorous plea using past experiences and said, **'We ate and drank in Your presence, and You taught in our streets.' But He will say, 'I tell you; I do not know where you are from."**

Two things stand out to me regarding those who play the part but are not part.

First, they say, **"We ate and drank in Your presence."** Their first claim is that they participated in his ministry by eating the fish and loaves. We were there! They spoke. Those were some very delicious sandwiches we had. They said we didn't turn your food away, except fish and bread!

The second claim was, **"You taught in our streets.'"** They said, look, Jesus, we not only ate your food, but we heard your inductive teachings, parables, powerful illustrations, etc. It is almost as ridiculous as saying, we sat through your sermons and prayer meetings, etc. - surely that counts for something.

To all this, Jesus replied, "I don't know you!" I don't recognize where you come from. I have seen you come in and out throughout your life, but you have never given your heart to Me. It comes and goes with you - so, no! I don't know you! Depart from Me!'

Depart from Me, all you workers of iniquity.'

To hear Jesus, say this to any one of us should scare us to the core of our spiritual being. To be rejected by the One who created us - should send chills down our spine.

Let us look at this a bit deeper as we close this devotion.

The word depart in Greek means to remove oneself. The Lord says to all who don't know Him, remove yourselves from me! You are workers of iniquity.

In other words, you loved yourself more than Me, you loved your ways more than Mine, and you preferred your plans more than Mine. Your interests, goals, and desires were first; I was second. Depart from Me, you workers of iniquity!

God help us all draw near to His heart and walk accordingly in His will and way. Neh'enah.

25

The Passion of God!

"Now there was a certain man of Ramathaim Zophim, of the mountains of Ephraim, and his name was Elkanah the son of Jeroham, the son of Elihu, the son of Tohu, the son of Zuph, an Ephraimite. And he had two wives: the name of one was Hannah, and the name of the other Peninnah. Peninnah had children, but Hannah had no children. This man went up from his city yearly to worship and sacrifice to the LORD of hosts in Shiloh. Also the two sons of Eli, Hophni and Phinehas, the priests of the LORD, were there. And whenever the time came for Elkanah to make an offering, he would give portions to Peninnah his wife and to all her sons and daughters. But to Hannah he would give a double portion, for he loved Hannah, although the LORD had closed her womb. And her rival also provoked her severely to make her miserable because the LORD had closed her womb. So it was, year by year, when she went up to the house of the LORD, that she provoked her; therefore she wept and did not eat. Then Elkanah her husband said to her, "Hannah, why do you weep? Why do you not eat? And why is your heart grieved? Am I not better to you than ten sons?" So Hannah arose after they had finished eating and drinking in Shiloh. Now Eli the priest was sitting on the seat by the doorpost of the tabernacle of the

LORD. And she was in bitterness of soul, and prayed to the LORD and wept in anguish. Then she made a vow and said, "O LORD of hosts, if You will indeed look on the affliction of Your maidservant and remember me, and not forget Your maidservant, but will give Your maidservant a male child, then I will give him to the LORD all the days of his life, and no razor shall come upon his head."** (1 Samuel 1:1-11)

As I read this powerful encounter between a desperate woman and God, I was moved deep within to understand the wisdom of the Lord in all of this. It seems to me that many things that are valuable to us don't happen automatically. We will have to fight (in prayer) for many important things!

Look at the story mentioned here and see where you and I fit in. I believe God speaks to us in this story and longs to see us position ourselves to get all that belongs to us.

Hannah and Peninnah

The story is about a man (Elkanah) who has two wives: Hannah and Peninnah. Hannah cannot have children, while Peninnah can.

Hannah's husband would go yearly to Shiloh to worship before the Lord, **"And whenever the time came for Elkanah to make an offering, he would give portions to**

Peninnah his wife, and to all her sons and daughters. But to Hannah he would give a double portion, for he loved Hannah, although the LORD had closed her womb."

Why would Elkanah give a double portion to his barren wife? Was it because he felt guilty or pity for his wife, Hannah? Whatever the case was, He didn't want Hannah to feel left out.

Provoked!

"And her rival also provoked her severely, to make her miserable, because the LORD had closed her womb. So it was, year by year, when she went up to the house of the LORD, that she provoked her; therefore, she wept and did not eat."

One of the things that I have found out in my walk with God is that when I have felt empty and useless, not to mention like a failure and unable to live out my values and convictions, there is a voice that comes to provoke me! What kind of voice is this? The word provoked in Hebrew means to be vexed, angry, or demoralized.

There is much to learn from this story. For one, Hannah was not feeling sorry for herself, or maybe she was, but her heart would not settle for the barrenness in her life. She was going to pursue her heart's passion.

Year after year, she went through the same emotions. Year after year, she would face Peninnah's mockery and condescending words. Hannah had had enough! This kind of provocation took her deeper and further than she had ever been. Finally, this one year, she just cried and lost her appetite!

Please notice that her husband tried to soothe her emotions but failed. He tried psychologically to get her to understand that he was better than ten sons. This didn't work.

You see, she wasn't looking for anything anyone could give her. She was looking for something that was burning from deep within. Why can't we understand this kind of stuff? We must get to where we yearn and are broken over what He wants us to do versus what we wish to accomplish.

Bitterness of Soul

"And she was in bitterness of soul and prayed to the LORD and wept in anguish." (I Samuel 1:10)

Part of the reason that our lives are not positioned in God is because (1) we don't see all that God has for us, and (2) we see it but don't have enough passion to go after it! It is here where God must raise someone or something to provoke us deep within, producing a violent desire to seek the heart of God with anguish.

The word anguish means bitter weeping! She couldn't contain herself anymore; she needed to hear from God. She needed the Lord to move on her behalf!

Have you ever been to this place?

The Vow!

"Then she made a vow and said, "O LORD of hosts, if You will indeed look on the affliction of Your maidservant and remember me, and not forget Your maidservant, but will give Your maidservant a male child, then I will give him to the LORD all the days of his life, and no razor shall come upon his head." (1 Samuel 1:11)

I think the Lord knew her longing all along. I believe God had been waiting for this woman to arrive at this particular place where she surrendered the one thing she felt she was missing from her life: her son.

We often don't enter God's fuller revelation, not because He doesn't want us to see or have it, but because He can't trust us with it just yet! Until we come to total desperation and anguish, He opens our spiritual womb and fulfills our heart's desires; it will happen when we genuinely vow it back to Him! Neh'enah.

David Mayorga

26

More and More!

"And this I pray, that your love may abound still more and more in knowledge and all discernment, that you may approve the things that are excellent, that you may be sincere and without offense till the day of Christ, being filled with the fruits of righteousness which are by Jesus Christ, to the glory and praise of God." (Philippians 1:9-11)

One of the things that I have observed in society is how people are fast starters but need better finishers. I have met many with great inspirations, but I need more strength to follow through with it! Have you noticed this? Perhaps this has happened to you at one point in your life, or maybe this has been your ongoing experience.

Why this happens to people can be argued or debated, but there is an excellent reason why some never finish.

Emotions Do Run Out of Steam.

In case you didn't know this, most inspirations are nothing more and nothing less than a ball of energy producing a fiery desire to pursue a worthy cause. You and I have been through this many times before.

It goes something like this:

We get inspiration from something we hear, see, or receive through teaching or godly revelation, and we immediately conclude that this is God's will for us. Yes, but is it?

Too often, we determine something to be God's will because of the momentum we feel or see. This is usually flesh in action. We embrace the wave just like seasoned surfers and ride it. Sometimes, we look spectacular riding the wave; other times, we look like fools.

We must realize that there are people who don't know the Spirit of God and don't recognize God's movement, mainly His voice; then there are those who perhaps are baby Christians who don't know any better and tend to lean on emotion rather than faith. This happens often.

The result is that if you have an inspiration and carry it through, you must answer the questions:

1. Was this inspiration birthed in the heart of God?

2. Was this an idea the Holy Spirit used to get me from point A to point B?

3. Can I give it back to God just like Abraham gave Isaac back to God on Mount Moriah? This is the test!

4. If I can surrender what God gave me back to God, I'm on my way to entering a life of surrender, a real life of faith.

More and More!

"And this I pray, that your love may abound still more and more in knowledge and all discernment, that you may approve the things that are excellent..."

When a man or woman of God develops an intimate relationship with God, it becomes their increasing passion. This becomes their reason for living, not church, but Jesus as a Person. If we don't fall in love with the Man Christ Jesus, we will fall in love with His creation. You cannot fall in love with a thing; you can only fall in love with a Person – that is Jesus!

Our fleshly conversations will always lean towards what we want and what we have done versus who He is and what He is leading us to do and speak. **Jesus said, "Most assuredly, I say to you, the Son can do nothing of Himself, but what He sees the Father do; for whatever He does, the Son also does in like manner."** (John 5:19)

Inspiration works to God's glory when it is given by the Spirit of God and kept by His fire. Otherwise, we won't have the power to keep that vision going; inspiration alone will not be enough to keep us through the character tests that await!

In closing, let me add briefly that the words more and more must not only be a cliché but a standard that we, as followers of Jesus, keep. After we receive revelation, knowledge, or instruction from the Holy Ghost, it is our duty as God's servants to pursue this awakening more and more!

Furthermore, we know we are fully responsible for positioning ourselves to hear God and follow through with what He has given us. May the Spirit of the Lord grant us the passion to follow Him more and more! Neh'enah.

27

God's Secret to True Greatness!

"He called a little child and had him stand among them. And he said: "I tell you the truth, unless you change and become like little children, you will never enter the kingdom of heaven. Therefore, whoever humbles himself like this child is the greatest in the kingdom of heaven." (Matthew 18:2-4 NIV)

When humanity thinks of greatness, it is usually related to position or status. People believe that receiving men's acceptance is a great thing; these people are enamored with promotions and reputations.

People naturally tend to compare themselves with peers and those surrounding them. For some odd reason, people feel better leading the pack versus following one. A spirit of competition to be first and outstanding dominates too many human beings.

When the Lord thinks of greatness, it is the direct opposite of man's motivations. God looks at greatness with a different value system. The Lord applauds humility and servanthood. According to the Scripture in James 4, it says, **"But He gives grace. Therefore, He says: "God resists the proud, but gives grace to the humble."** Here, we find what God is genuinely into.

Let us dive into God's heart regarding this great subject of greatness and look at it from God's perspective.

The Truth!

"He called a little child and had him stand among them. And he said: "I tell you the truth..."

As Jesus took the little child and had him stand among the people, He began to expound a great truth about the kingdom of God to all those present. It would be beneficial to lend our hearts to this and embrace the secret of becoming great in God's eyes.

Jesus called it a truth. What does truth mean? Well, for starters, the truth is not a lie. Jesus said, "I'm not going to lie to you, but allow you to see how things are. He took the opportunity to present this heavenly truth with an earthly example.

Unless You Change!

Jesus took the opportunity to bring this child and say to all those present, **" Unless you change and become like little children, you will never enter the kingdom of God."**

When Jesus said unless you change, what did He mean?

The word change in the original Greek means *"cause to rotate as on an axis, i.e., on the potter's wheel. Another definition is to turn it upside down or over by digging or plowing."*

Jesus told those present: *"Unless you are changed from what you presently are or from the way you think; unless your life is transformed (being on the potter's wheel), you will have no access into the kingdom of God."*

To access God, one must be born-again – this is what Jesus told Nicodemus in John 3. We can't see or enter the kingdom of God in our old nature from Adam; we must become a new creation in Christ. (see 2 Corinthians 5:17)

What Does It Mean to Have No Access to the Kingdom?

Having no access to the kingdom of God means that you don't have a way to understand the laws and keys of God's kingdom. Not only do they need to be spiritually discerned, but they must also be apprehended by faith. It is not enough to hear truth; one must walk it out also!

Jesus challenged all religious followers with this illustration, making it a principle of life and a matter of the heart when He said, "Therefore, whoever humbles himself like this child is the greatest in the kingdom of heaven."

Humility!

The condition of the heart must always be one of humility. Without humility in the heart, there will be no access to God. One must realize this. Jesus used a little child to exemplify the spirit that God requires for access. Unless one is as gentle and soft-hearted as a child, he will have no way to connect with God. This is all the Lord Jesus was trying to convey.

The interesting thing about this exchange was why Jesus would make this an issue. I am sure He could see through the religious pride of the crowd and proceed to educate them on kingdom matters.

Pride and arrogance would be the opposite of humility; therefore, Jesus set Himself to teach this eternal principle. There is no way anyone would get near God without humility; thus, He awakened their conscience and intellect. This is mercy in action!

As I close this devotion, please know that it is God's heart for His children to continue with a humble heart before Him. Greatness in His eyes is found here! Humility will forever be the model God looks for in any vessel that wears His Name. Neh'enah.

28

Valuable Seeds of the Kingdom!

"And when a great multitude had gathered, and they had come to Him from every city, He spoke by a parable: "A sower went out to sow his seed. And as he sowed, some fell by the wayside; and it was trampled down, and the birds of the air devoured it. Some fell on rock; and as soon as it sprang up, it withered away because it lacked moisture. And some fell among thorns, and the thorns sprang up with it and choked it. But others fell on good ground, sprang up, and yielded a crop a hundredfold." When He had said these things He cried, "He who has ears to hear, let him hear!" Then His disciples asked Him, saying, "What does this parable mean?" And He said, "To you, it has been given to know the mysteries of the kingdom of God, but to the rest, it is given in parables, that
'Seeing they may not see,
And hearing they may not understand.'
"Now the parable is this: The seed is the word of God. Those by the wayside are the ones who hear; then the devil comes and takes away the word out of their hearts, lest they should believe and be saved. But the ones on the rock are those who, when they hear, receive the word with joy; and these have no root, who believe for a while and in time of temptation fall away. Now, the ones that

fell among thorns are those who, when they have heard, go out and are choked with cares, riches, and pleasures of life and bring no fruit to maturity. But the ones that fell on the good ground are those who, having heard the word with a noble and good heart, keep it and bear fruit with patience." (Luke 8:4-15)

One of the most valuable principles I have learned in my pursuit of God is this: When God gets ready to change the course of our present state, He will begin this by sowing seeds of the kingdom in us.

Seeds always symbolize something new, a new beginning, a new process, etc. Always look out for these experiences as the Lord makes way to start something fresh in us. Remember, He begins with a seed.

Everything We Need is In the Seed!

One thing we must remember is that everything we need for the upcoming season is found in the seed. If the seed God is attempting to plant in us finds its mark, it will bring forth all God has intended for us.

Remember that all we need for the next season will be in that seed, and once planted in our hearts, we must do everything in our power to cultivate it, protect it, and take full responsibility for it until it comes to maturity and brings forth fruit.

Please understand that cultivating a fresh seed in us is not the same as simply keeping up with church life. It is not the same as offering ministry to the lost or helping the ministry in various ways – cultivating a seed is more than mere service! It is a life of cultivation, and one must walk in new levels of humility and brokenness.

The Sower's Intent: Four Different Hearts & Experiences

It is the Father's will to sow seeds of life into us. Seeds that will develop our lives into a greater fullness of who He is. So, the Lord sets Himself to sow seed…

The first seed that the sower tried sowing "**… fell by the wayside, and it was trampled down, and the birds of the air devoured it."** In the natural, this means very little; only a farmer will calculate its loss, but in the Spirit, this means that **"Those by the wayside are the ones who hear; then the devil comes and takes away the word out of their hearts, lest they should believe and be saved.**

The second seed fell by the rocks: **"Some fell on rock; and as soon as it sprang up, it withered away because it lacked moisture."** Naturally, this seed had little hope of surviving because it lacked moisture. I think the heat killed it when the sun finally came up. In the Spirit, this means that "**…the ones on the rock are those who, when they hear, receive the word with joy; and these have no root, who believe for a while and in time of temptation**

fall away." If any seed doesn't have a root, it won't live for long. Once the time of testing comes, they will fall away!

The third seed fell among thorns, **"And some fell among thorns, and the thorns sprang up with it and choked it."** Some things surround us that are not good for us to be around. We must discern what these things are and get ready to fight them. In the Spirit of the Lord, Jesus said that these seeds that fell among thorns **"...are those who, when they have heard, go out and are choked with cares, riches, and pleasures of life, and bring no fruit to maturity."**

If we aren't expecting a battle or think that Christian living is not about spiritual warfare, we will be targets for the enemy, and due to our lack of discipline, we will succumb to the devil's tactics and schemes.

Finally, Jesus said that the fourth seed fell on good ground. **"But others fell on good ground, sprang up, and yielded a crop a hundredfold."** The sower found some good soil and planted the seed. It produced bountifully.

Our hearts must be ready to receive seed from God. We must always be attentive to God planting seeds in us and be prepared to accept, protect, and cultivate all God is doing. Jesus said that the fourth seed fell on good soil, representing in the spirit **"...those who, having heard the word with a noble and good heart, keep it and bear fruit with**

patience."

If we take care of all that God gives us, we will mature and grow and produce good fruit – in this, the Father will be glorified. Neh'enah.

Volume 8

29

Nothing is Greater Than God!

"Now Eliab, his oldest brother, heard when he spoke to the men, and Eliab's anger was aroused against David, and he said, "Why did you come down here? And with whom have you left those few sheep in the wilderness? I know your pride and the insolence of your heart, for you have come down to see the battle." And David said, "What have I done now? Is there not a cause?" Then he turned from him toward another and said the same thing, and these people answered him as the first ones did. Now, when the words that David spoke were heard, they reported them to Saul, and he sent for him. Then David said to Saul, "Let no man's heart fail because of him; your servant will go and fight with this Philistine." And Saul said to David, "You are not able to go against this Philistine to fight with him; for you are a youth, and he a man of war from his youth." But David said to Saul, "Your servant used to keep his father's sheep, and when a lion or a bear came and took a lamb out of the flock, I went out after it and struck it, and delivered the lamb from its mouth; and when it arose against me, I caught it by its beard, and struck and killed it. Your servant has killed both lion and bear; and this uncircumcised Philistine will be like one of them, seeing he has defied the armies of the living God." Moreover, David said, "The

LORD, who delivered me from the paw of the lion and from the paw of the bear, He will deliver me from the hand of this Philistine." And Saul said to David, "Go, and the LORD be with you!" (1 Samuel 17:28-37)

Israel in a Crisis

We pick up our story of Israel finding itself in a great battle against the Philistines. There always seemed to be some battle going on with the Philistines.

This battle had a little difference; the Philistines had a secret weapon, apparently so powerful that Israel had never seen. This weapon was called Goliath! This giant of man was so tall and robust that it made Israel tremble.

Israel had faced challenges before but had never confronted a giant face-to-face, as far as we know. I'm sure they had seen giants before but had never been challenged by his words.

Yes, the crisis was severe, and the problem was now!

This giant was so frightening that Israel trembled in their boots. People ran from him, and this caused their leaders, not to mention King Saul, to be in disarray.

In the center of a fear-controlled army during this chaos, God was about to change the course of history. The problem was Goliath; the answer to that problem was David.

God Has a Man in Mind – David!

David was the youngest of his family, and God had anointed him to be a great leader someday. The time had not come for him to be king yet, but his opportunity to step into something greater than himself had arrived.

David was a shepherd boy and was tending to his father's sheep. As he went about his business, his father told him one day to take food to his brothers in the Valley of Elah, for they were in battle against the Philistines.

As David reached the army arrayed for battle, he saw and heard Goliath threaten Israel and defy them.

David was offended by the giant's words, and in essence, David said, who does this man think he is defying the armies of Israel?

David was furious about how anyone would dare stand against God's army.

Overcoming Jealousy from Those Around You.

As little David inquired what reward a man would receive if he killed this giant, his older brother intervened and rebuked David. He told David that this was not his business and that he should return home and care for the sheep.

I believe that too many people in leadership can't recognize God's faith in their followers. They don't know that God can use anyone who trusts God. The brother didn't like the attention David was getting from his words, so he rebuked him. In all this, David was adamant about killing Goliath.

Dare to Believe God!

"Then David said to Saul, "Let no man's heart fail because of him; your servant will go and fight with this Philistine."

David took it upon himself to make some powerful statements to those around him that the word got to King Saul, **"Now when the words which David spoke were heard, they reported them to Saul; and he sent for him. Then David told Saul, "Let no man's heart fail because of him; your servant will go and fight with this Philistine."**

David was bold and full of faith. Listen to his boldness: **"Let no man's heart fail because of him!"** Ponder this for a bit: He is a lowly shepherd; he has no training in battle; He is young and inexperienced – this is nothing more than a recipe for getting beat up by this experienced monster. Knowing that all these things were facts, David still concludes his statement and says, **"…your servant**

will go and fight with this Philistine!" David was determined. He knew the secret that most people don't know: He knew God!

King Saul Discourages David!

"And Saul said to David, "You cannot go against this Philistine to fight with him; for you are a youth, and he a man of war from his youth."

If something usually happens when faith takes wings, it is that fear always follows up with some commonsense reason why things are impossible to accomplish or countless excuses of why something can't be done! I know you have heard or experienced this in your own life.

King Saul's political career was probably at the lowest ratings, and he needed something to increase his credibility. Now, David knew that God's army was not going to fight. He knew they were overcome by fear and stepped up to the opportunity.

It only took one external look from King Saul and concluded, **"You cannot go against this Philistine to fight with him…"** He then explains why You are too young, David, and you have no battle experience. As good as these two facts were, we must remember the God factor. There is always a battle between the natural and the supernatural.

Wherever God is, victory is assured. God, and at least one man who believes Him, are always the majority in any fight!

David's Resumé

"But David said to Saul, "Your servant used to keep his father's sheep, and when a lion or a bear came and took a lamb out of the flock, I went out after it and struck it, and delivered the lamb from its mouth; and when it arose against me, I caught it by its beard, and struck and killed it. Your servant has killed both lion and bear; and this uncircumcised Philistine will be like one of them, seeing he has defied the armies of the living God. Moreover, David said, "The LORD, who delivered me from the paw of the lion and from the paw of the bear, He will deliver me from the hand of this Philistine."

After hearing King Saul state his lack of battle experience and age, David gives out his battle experience resumé.

In short, David tells King Saul, **"Your servant used to keep his father's sheep, and when a lion or a bear came and took a lamb out of the flock, I went out after it and struck it, and delivered the lamb from its mouth; and when it arose against me, I caught it by its beard, and struck and killed it. Your servant has killed both lion and bear; and this uncircumcised Philistine will be like one of them, seeing he has defied the armies of the living God."**

In my service unto the Lord, I believe that the life of faith is marked by the revelation of how big and great God is. The problem, the crises, or the challenge can be as high as the sky, but who is bigger than God, the Creator of the universe? If you see the Lord as the all-powerful God that He is, who can outpower him? And if God is for you, who can be against you? Enough said.

David was a man of this caliber. He knew Goliath was big, but He knew God was bigger!

David would not be swayed from accomplishing this: Goliath didn't scare him, his brother Eliab didn't convince him, and King Saul couldn't quench the fire within him. Instead, David got the blessing from King Saul, **"Go, and the Lord be with you!"**

In being a servant of God, you will have many mountains to climb; some are higher than others, but always remember, nothing is higher than God! He is on your side and will see you through in any circumstance. Neh'enah.

30

Visitations from the Lord! - Part 1

"Now, as He drew near, He saw the city and wept over it, saying, "If you had known, even you, especially in this your day, the things that make for your peace! But now they are hidden from your eyes. For days will come upon you when your enemies will build an embankment around you, surround you and close you in on every side, and level you, and your children within you, to the ground; and they will not leave in you one stone upon another, because you did not know the time of your visitation." (Luke 19:41-44)

The coming of Christ into the world was the Father's perfect will. In His coming, Christ spoke of the Kingdom of God and described it creatively. He used parables to connect with the people heaven's truths. Some people understood God's heart, but most were at a loss for words.

Apart from teaching and expounding God's thoughts and love to the countless multitudes, Jesus also laid out God's eternal plan. In doing this, Jesus took it a step further and taught them about their future in Him if they abide in Him. The peace, the joy, and the power of an endless life would be theirs if they only believed.

Many who heard Christ's words were critical of these truths. They didn't accept Christ or His teachings, mainly the Pharisees and the different religious groups during the days of Jesus. The Jews were attentive to keeping the laws, the holidays, and even the rituals were kept systematically, but Christ Jesus, the Son of God, was never accepted.

Is it any wonder why Christ carried such a burden for lost humanity? He left His throne in heaven so He would live among His own, but His own didn't receive Him. Can you imagine this heartbreak? God knew that humanity needed Christ, but they didn't know their spiritual poverty. It's not much different today!

Yet with all these facts, Christ didn't hold back from giving His life away; he gave it as a ransom for all humanity. The Scripture says **"…for the joy that was set before him endured the cross…"** (Hebrews 12:2). Jesus went ALL OUT for you and me!

The Jews Missed It!

In the text above, Christ came to Jerusalem and said, **"If you had known, even you, especially in this your day, the things that make for your peace!"** The price to pay for not seeing Christ was hefty and still a hefty one. Without Christ, no one can find life, the meaning of it, or the keeping of it. Life without Christ is a lifeless experience.

It is crucial to understand that the Lord not only visited His people but still visited His servants by His Spirit. He still comes to us and leads us.

In the text we just read in Luke 19:41-44, we find that Jesus was broken over the fact that His people (the Jews) had just missed an opportunity to know the One true God. Access to God's throne was before them, and they didn't see or acknowledge it. This is very sad and very consequential.

Jesus said, **"For days will come upon you when your enemies will build an embankment around you, surround you and close you in on every side, and level you, and your children within you, to the ground; and they will not leave in you one stone upon another, because you did not know the time of your visitation."**

Why Is It Valuable to Recognize His Visitations?

I believe God's servants must always do what they can to be in tune with God and His Spirit. We cannot afford to go through life without revelation, knowledge, and prophetic insight.

The Christian religion generally teaches God's Word with formality. Don't get me wrong, I'm all for formality and correct theology. It is the lack of Holy Spirit revelation that irks me! Religion tends to focus on God's literal, logos word; it usually isn't experiential.

People full of the Holy Spirit experience God at a higher level. There is no doubt about that. We need this understanding in our being. God will come and invade a man's heart and mind if we so desire.

Let me make a point: We need His Word and proper theology, and we must also embrace the Spirit's revelatory anointing, the prophetic.

You see, others are filled with the Spirit of God and have discovered the gifts of the Spirit. They have realized that God's Spirit still speaks and moves in their midst. God's prophetic anointing makes the words of God come alive (Rhema). Those in tune with God's Spirit or seeking a personal visitation will eventually receive one.

God's visitations are so needed today as our world continues to change. We will learn that history has a way of repeating itself, and we will do well to pay attention to our forefathers. Knowing how they navigated through change and how the Spirit and the Word led them through history at every turn is a key we must understand.

We must do what we can to stay in God's word and in tune with God's visitations – whether corporate or personal.

Let us open our spiritual eyes and lend our spiritual ears to hear His voice in this hour. Neh'enah.

31

Visitations from the Lord! - Part 2

"Then the LORD saw that the wickedness of man was great in the earth and that every intent of the thoughts of his heart was only evil continually. And the LORD was sorry that He had made man on the earth, and He was grieved in His heart. So, the LORD said, "I will destroy man whom I have created from the face of the earth, both man and beast, creeping thing and birds of the air, for I am sorry that I have made them." But Noah found grace in the eyes of the LORD...". (Genesis 6:5-8)

This is the genealogy of Noah. Noah was a just man, perfect in his generation. Noah walked with God." (Genesis 6:9)

And God said to Noah, "The end of all flesh has come before Me, for the earth is filled with violence through them; and behold, I will destroy them with the earth." (Genesis 6:13)

By faith Noah, being divinely warned of things not yet seen, moved with godly fear, prepared an ark for the saving of his household...". (Hebrews 11:7)

When God, by His Spirit, visits us, it is usually to speak

and direct our lives. He brings awareness to us and downloads vital instructions for the coming season in our lives. His revelation may come as a warning, an appeal, or a command.

Until I'm Satisfied!

The key to hearing God is to discern what He is saying to me. What is His Spirit causing my inner man to behold, learn, or do? We must ask ourselves these questions until our hearts are satisfied with the answer. This is one of the ways to know that we have received what the Lord has in store for us.

When the Lord visits us, we must always be open to hearing Him. Our preferences, biases, and views must be put on hold, and sometimes, they must be discarded from our minds. The Lord desires to speak, and He wants full attention from us. We must know this beforehand.

It All Begins with God's Desires

The Scripture above states, **"And the LORD was sorry that He had made man on the earth, and He was grieved in His heart."**

God's emotions can be seen all through the Scriptures. His joy, anger, desire, zeal, and passion for lost humanity can all be seen, heard, or felt. At this point in history, man's thoughts and intents of his heart were evil, and God was sorry that He had made man.

What does the word sorry mean? It means regret or to change one's mind.

The Lord felt differently now that men had perverted themselves. God was about to unleash His fury, but not before finding someone He could trust to help Him in His plan. He chose Noah.

God Visits Noah!

"And God said to Noah, "The end of all flesh has come before Me, for the earth is filled with violence through them; and behold, I will destroy them with the earth."

In this conversation, God pours His heart to Noah and allows him to feel the fury He is feeling. Can you imagine this? Noah was qualified to hear God's wrath! This should make us wonder what we are prepared for.

After God got Noah's attention, the Lord shared his plan with Noah. It was simple, but would Noah obey? **The Lord said, "Make yourself an ark of gopherwood…"** (Genesis 6:14a).

In this visitation, the Lord expressed His desire with Noah; along with the willingness, God also shared His intent and what part Noah would play in this plan.

One thing I have noticed about God's visitations with humanity is that most, if not all, moves of God begin in God's heart, and we get to share in those emotions. Our visitations are always connected in some form or another with God's emotions.

Responding to God!

The visitation of God that Noah experienced required an immediate response! Noah was told that a flood would be coming and that he needed to build this ark soon. Time was of the essence.

All visitations from the Lord are intended to move us upward in God. Always remember this.

The Scripture says that after Noah heard the Lord's warning, he, **"By faith Noah, being divinely warned of things not yet seen, moved with godly fear, prepared an ark for the saving of his household…"**.

God's visitation demands action! To the degree that you know God is to the degree that you will move. If we don't know God, we won't have urgency. If we truly know the Father, we will even give our lives for Him!

With all the information downloaded into his spirit, Noah

moved with godly fear. God's visitations will always be entwined with our knowledge of Him. As A.W. Tozer so eloquently wrote, God Tells Those Who Care! Neh'enah.

32

Visitations from the Lord! - Part 3

"And he arose that night and took his two wives, his two female servants, and his eleven sons, and crossed over the ford of Jabbok. He took them, sent them over the brook, and sent over what he had. Then Jacob was left alone; and a Man wrestled with him until the breaking of day. Now when He saw that He did not prevail against him, He touched the socket of his hip; and the socket of Jacob's hip was out of joint as He wrestled with him. And He said, "Let Me go, for the day breaks."
But he said, "I will not let You go unless You bless me!"
So, He said to him, "What is your name?"
He said, "Jacob."
And He said, "Your name shall no longer be called Jacob, but Israel; for you have struggled with God and with men and have prevailed."
Then Jacob asked, saying, "Tell me Your name, I pray."
And He said, "Why is it that you ask about My name?" And He blessed him there.
So, Jacob called the name of the place Peniel: "For I have seen God face to face, and my life is preserved." Just as he crossed over Penuel the sun rose on him, and he limped on his hip." (Genesis 32:22-31)

In defining our Christian walk, we usually come into

God's kingdom when we accept God in our hearts. Our walk with God is an exciting one. As we try to pick up a bible and start reading, we learn about God's attributes and character. We read countless stories that testify to God's working power among His creation, etc. Until now, Christianity is an excellent, clean-cut religion that seems to add value to our lives and those around us.

No Pain, No Gain!

Then it happens….

A preacher or teacher speaks on commitment and the need for discipline. Another series of stories shows how the believer must carry his cross and die daily in his fleshly ways. The challenge continues to rise when you are asked to provide a tenth of all your income and attend the weekly prayer meeting.

Soon, one of the brothers or sisters will ask you to join their discipleship cell group. You begin to get pushed around (spiritually speaking); in truth, no one is making you, but you may feel this way. The group leader went deeper and told the group we would start a 21-day fast this week. Make sure that you get ready for this.

Suddenly, you begin to ask yourself, "Why do I have to read my Bible daily, pray daily, give of myself to God, and die daily, not to mention that I can't eat for 21 days?

Why?"

What is Happening to Me?

If you feel like this in your walk with God, let me tell you, the Lord is visiting you. What is the reason? God has visited you to show you what He doesn't like about you and what He wants you to become! In other words, God has brought you into a process of transformation.

The Breaking of the Old Man

The story above talks to us about our forefather, Jacob. This man is given over to stealing and supplanting others; this is his character. It comes from the Old Testament and means "supplanter," often interpreted as someone who seizes, circumvents, or usurps.

Jacob had ripped off his brother Esau of his birthright, among many other things. This got Jacob in a lot of trouble. This speaks to us of our old nature and our carnal way of being until God begins the process of breaking the old man.

One of the things that I believe the church must come back to these days is the preaching of holiness. The message of holiness says, God saved you; now lend yourself to the Lord so that He may show you His ways. Surrender and yield yourself to Him and allow your body to be used as an instrument, not only for worship, but to manifest the gospel of the kingdom to God and the world around you. I believe this is the high calling of God in Christ Jesus.

Prevailing with God!

And He said, "Your name shall no longer be called Jacob, but Israel; for you have struggled with God and men and have prevailed."

Just as Jacob wrestled with a Man (Jesus Christ), we must wrestle with God until He transforms us. It is not until our name is changed that we enter God's perfect will.

I firmly believe that unless God comes and visits us and pierces us with the arrow of His holiness message, we won't enter God's high calling in Christ Jesus.

Let us give ourselves time to recognize His visitation. It might be the most significant move of God for us yet! Neh'enah.

33

A *Burning Bush* Calling!

"Now Moses was tending the flock of Jethro his father-in-law, the priest of Midian. And he led the flock to the back of the desert, and came to Horeb, the mountain of God. And the Angel of the LORD appeared to him in a flame of fire from the midst of a bush. So, he looked, and behold, the bush was burning with fire, but the bush was not consumed. Then Moses said, "I will now turn aside and see this great sight, why the bush does not burn." So, when the LORD saw that he turned aside to look, God called to him from the midst of the bush and said, "Moses, Moses!" And he said, "Here I am." Then He said, "Do not draw near this place. Take your sandals off your feet, for the place where you stand is holy ground." Moreover, He said, "I am the God of your father—the God of Abraham, the God of Isaac, and the God of Jacob." And Moses hid his face, for he was afraid to look upon God." (Exodus 3:1-6)

While spending some excellent quality time in God's presence, the Spirit of the Lord gave me a vision of a small flame burning amid darkness. The small flame was burning ever so intently.

Now, in this vision, there are a few things of interest. One of these things is that the flame was so small that I could hardly identify it. I had to put my eyeglasses so I could see it! As I paid attention, I saw the flickering flame burning brightly.

The second thing I saw was the great darkness. Immediately, my mind concluded that the darkness was the wicked world system and demonic oppression that surrounded us. To all this, the Spirit of God corrected me and said, "David, this is not what this vision is!" So, the Lord began to show me…

Darkness in Disguise!

The Spirit of God told me this: The small, unquenchable flame is your ministry. The darkness was not this present world but the church's spiritual condition. I have raised you as a burning bush in the last days of ministry. Your calling is divine and burns alone amid this religious world, which is nothing more than darkness in disguise!

Nothing awakens this present darkness like the fire of God. I have called you from long ago to be this for my glory. Many things will always attempt to hush, quiet, destroy, eradicate, erase, take away, turn off, shut off the fire I have placed in your soul. So long as you draw near to Me, you will never lack this holy fire. Always remember, this is not about you, but about Me! Now go, for I have sent you, saith the Lord.

What is a Burning Bush Calling?

We can look at the text above in Exodus 3:1-6 to clarify this calling. As many of us have read the story of Moses and the burning bush experience, we must first realize that God had this intention in His heart to deliver His people from slavery at the hands of Pharaoh. Jehovah God raised and called Moses for this hour to answer prayer.

Moses had been trained in Egypt for about 40 years, if you remember. Then killed a man and was now wanted by Pharaoh. So, Moses fled to the desert to hide for 40 years. Moses was now to be trained by God in the ways of the desert, and by the way, these are God's training methods. He will get the man alone and establish him in the loneliest parts of the earth.

Burning Bush Calling Begins Here . . .

One day, while taking care of his father-in-law's sheep, Moses encountered a strange sight: a bush that was burning, but it wasn't being consumed. As Moses drew near this bush, God spoke from within the bush and said to Moses, **"Moses, Moses!" And he said, "Here I am." Then He said, "Do not draw near this place."**

An encounter with God is the first step in this ministry calling. God must meet with you face-to-face before anything can be established.

Secondly, the flesh will be apprehended at the door. Moses thought He could get a better peek at this miraculous sight, but the Lord stopped him cold! He told him not to come any closer! This is the place where God knocks all the silliness out of us.

Thirdly, Moses was asked not to step into a deeper dimension with God if he wasn't willing to take off his sandals. Here's what the Lord said: **"Take your sandals off your feet, for the place where you stand is holy ground."** Holy ground is a spiritual condition where God brings us so that we may surrender our rights. Removing one's sandals represented the yielding of personal rights. Unless we yield our rights to God [see Galatians 2:20,] He can't and won't use us!

Fourthly, the holy ground is a place of fire. Those who live in it are full of the fire of God. Unless the vessel of God is willing to enter by removing their sandals, they can't join the holy ground. To live outside of holy ground is the equivalent as if one is living to please and appease the flesh! A burning bush calling or ministry is unpopular with organized, traditional, or user-friendly religions.

Finally, a realization of the holiness of God. **"Moreover, He said, "I am the God of your father—the God of Abraham, the God of Isaac, and the God of Jacob." And Moses hid his face, for he was afraid to look upon God."** Once Moses heard that it was indeed God speaking and challenging him to take off his sandals, Moses knew that he had crossed over.

I believe that God is raising a people who carry this same desire and anointing in the body of Christ. May the Lord continue to burn in us the desire to meet with Him daily! I genuinely don't believe that anything less than this holy ground calling will do if we are to survive the onslaught that is coming upon this nation and the nations of the world in the not-so-distant future. Neh'enah.

34

At the Scent of Water!

"For there is hope for a tree,
If it is cut down, that it will sprout again,
And that its tender shoots will not cease.
Though its root may grow old in the earth,
And its stump may die in the ground,
Yet, at the scent of water, it will bud.
And bring forth branches like a plant." (Job 14:7-11)

"Leave no [such] room or foothold for the devil [give no opportunity to him]." (Ephesians 4:27)

While browsing at one of our local retail stores, I heard an old song through the store's speakers. It was an old familiar song I have heard many times called "I Put a Spell on You" by the 70's rock group Credence Clearwater Revival. I wouldn't say I like the song, but I want you to read these few lyrics from it song:

*"I put a spell on you because you're mine
You better stop the thing that you're doin'."*

Hearing it all the way through as I made my way through the store's aisles, the Spirit of the Lord came to me and began to unfold something to me.

Is the Old Man Truly Dead?

As I pondered the words of this song, a thought entered my mind. Is the carnal man indeed yielded and fully surrendered to God? I asked myself, "How would I know someone put a spell on me if I wasn't told?" How can anyone bewitch me if I don't mind it?" How can I be fearful of something that has not entered my natural mind, of course, unless it did enter?

Can you see what I am saying? Our minds (flesh) capture pictures related to man's fallen nature. The more we focus on these pictures and words, the more the flesh awakens to the reality of these thoughts. Do you see it?

When we hear the Apostle Paul saying, **"Likewise you also, reckon yourselves to be dead indeed to sin, but alive to God in Christ Jesus our Lord,"** he is saying, give no life to sin!

In other words, the flesh depends on our paying mind to it. So long as we don't give it life, it remains lifeless! If we open our natural faculties for the carnal man to be revived, he will. The natural man responds to a particular sound or frequency that enters through sight, hearing, touching, or tasting.

We can walk in the Spirit's power and be fully anointed for one minute, and then encounter frequencies in our lower nature that will plant ideas or thoughts that will challenge the very words of God. Is it any wonder why the great Apostle Paul reveals to us about spiritual warfare and says in 2 Corinthians 10:4-5, **"For the weapons of our warfare are not carnal but mighty in God for pulling down strongholds, casting down arguments and every high thing that exalts itself against the knowledge of God, bringing every thought into captivity to the obedience of Christ...".**

At the Scent of Water

Like the tree that is fallen, and rotting can be revived by the scent of water, so is the flesh.

I have heard people speak very foolishly due to their immaturity in the things of God, who end up cursing people or condemning people simply because they don't know what they don't know.

How would I know someone hates me if I was never told that? How do I know that a witch wants to curse me if no one ever tells me? The other question would be, "Why would I want to know that someone hates me when I already know that the spirit of this world hates Christ? If I'm in Christ, I must already know I am not wanted! I should know that the world desires to crucify me! Jesus said, **"If the world hates you, you know that it hated Me before it hated you. If you were of the world, the world would**

love its own. Yet because you are not of the world, but I chose you out of the world, therefore the world hates you." (John 15:18-19)

My concern is not who hates me, who despises me, or who wants to crucify my life. My concern should always be, am I walking daily in the power of the Spirit? Am I keeping the flesh under submission to the Holy Ghost? Am I pleasing God with my life?

Leave No Room for the Devil!

Paul writes to the Ephesians to be aware of not leaving any footholds (opportunities) to the devil to do his dirty work. We do have control over that. Putting ourselves in situations that will hurt us is not wise. The devil can't do anything to us if we don't present opportunities. The call to walk in the Spirit could not be greater these days!

Remember, the flesh will arise at the scent of water (carnal frequencies through carnal faculties). If you feed the mind with negativity, fear, doubt, ungodly thoughts, and opinions that are opposite of God's will, they will have an impact on our souls. Neh'enah.

35

God Shares Secrets with Those Closest to Him!

"The secret [of the sweet, satisfying companionship] of the Lord have they who fear (revere and worship) Him, and He will show them His covenant and reveal to them its [deep, inner] meaning." (Psalm 25:14. AMP)

"It happened after this that David inquired of the LORD, saying, "Shall I go up to any of the cities of Judah?"
And the LORD said to him, "Go up."
David said, "Where shall I go up?"
And He said, "To Hebron." (2 Samuel 2:1)

During a time of great transition, David inquired of the Lord, for Saul and Jonathan had been killed, and things looked grim in Israel.

One thing to note is that whenever we find ourselves amid difficulty or don't know what is happening around us, it has become my conviction and now more of a practical thing to inquire of the Lord.

The Lord knows everything about me, my life, present, and future. He will disclose His heart and mind to me – I wholeheartedly believe this! So, why not go after His counsel and find my way around life's most challenging moments?

Now, David was a true lover of God. He wasn't a wishy-washy follower or a pretender. He believed God and was fully assured that God had him and would lead Him accordingly. Do you have this conviction?

What makes a man have this type of confidence in God? What makes Him so sure that God will come through for him?

Though there may be many factors or elements to this, nothing compares with the simple acts of yielding, surrendering, and allowing God to be first in all things. This is not a gift; this is a character trait! You can only grow in it by doing it!

Intimacy!

This walk with God is perhaps better understood as an intimate walk with the Creator. To walk with God and allow Him to have preeminence in your life guarantees an open highway of revelation. Downloads of knowledge that are beyond one's life can be received.

In the Oxford Dictionary of Language, the word intimacy means close familiarity or friendship, closeness. Wikipedia defines intimacy as involving an intimate, personal association and belonging together. It is a familiar and very close affective connection due to a bond formed through knowledge and experience of the other. Genuine intimacy in human relationships requires dialogue, transparency, vulnerability, and reciprocity.

David was undoubtedly an intimate lover of Jehovah God. All that David was hoping to become was wrapped up in God's desires, not his own.

Intimacy takes Work!

To become intimate lovers of God, we must understand the definition and follow the steps that get us there. Becoming an intimate lover of God is a bit harder than what people say or bible teachers teach. There must be a certain amount of discipline to make it happen. Let us dive in…

Dialogue. There must be dialogue with God. If you want to build any friendship, there must be communication with that individual; it is the same with God. We must desire to talk and dialogue with God from our innermost being. Converse with Him about anything and everything that concerns you. Here's the secret: Everything that concerns you concerns Him!

Transparency. Secondly, we must become transparent. We must open our hearts to the Lord and allow Him to hear our deepest longings, fears, insecurities, worries, etc. The

Lord takes delight in it. Here's another secret to intimacy: When we open our hearts to God, not only do we allow our spirit to touch Him, but His Spirit touches ours! This will make all the difference in our connection with God.

Vulnerability. What does it mean to be vulnerable? For starters, to be vulnerable refers to "the quality or state of being exposed to the possibility of being attacked or harmed, either physically or emotionally." A window of vulnerability is a time frame within which defensive measures are diminished, compromised, or lacking.

When a person is vulnerable before God, that individual confesses before the Lord, " I am at your mercy, God, and if you don't hold me, support me, or carry me, I will not make it alone! " What a beautiful place to be in God!

There is a Scripture that comes to mind here:

"To you I lift up my eyes,
   O you who are enthroned in the heavens!
   Behold, as the eyes of servants
   look to the hand of their master,
as the eyes of a maidservant
   to the hand of her mistress,
so our eyes look to the Lord our God,
   till he has mercy upon us." (Psalm 123:1, 2)

Reciprocity. Finally, reciprocity is needed to go deeper in this relationship with God. What is reciprocity? In social psychology, reciprocity is a social norm of responding to a positive action with another positive action, rewarding kind actions.

As the Lord begins to touch your heart with His love, you respond to Him using your heart. As He gives you, you give Him. You will discover that your life will begin to mirror His as you become one with Him! The more He loves you, the more you love Him, the more He loves you, and so forth. Do you see it?

Whatever it takes, my dear friend, with all your strength, seek intimacy with God. I believe intimacy is God's higher calling in Christ Jesus. As good as great works are, as important as winning souls is, nothing is more excellent than knowing God intimately! Neh'enah.

36

Disappointed?

"Now behold, two of them were traveling that same day to a village called Emmaus, which was seven miles from Jerusalem. And they talked together of all these things which had happened. So it was, while they conversed and reasoned, that Jesus Himself drew near and went with them. But their eyes were restrained, so that they did not know Him. And He said to them, "What kind of conversation is this that you have with one another as you walk and are sad?" (Luke 24:13-17)

Can you picture this scenario: Two eyewitnesses to the crucifixion of Christ who are heading back home yes in disappointment, but why? Allow me the time to share these thoughts that the Spirit of God shared.

In the text above, the word left by Luke says that they conversed and reasoned. The word reasoned in this text means to examine with, together, or to dispute.

So, these two men had been right there at the scene when Christ was hung on the cross; they saw Him die! It doesn't get much more accurate than that. They were broken-hearted and beyond reasoning.

So, disappointment and confusion flooded their souls for the next seven miles as they went home. The more they reasoned, the more disappointed they grew, and so on.

Can you see what is happening here? Can you feel the pain of these two servants of Christ? Imagine being told that you will inherit the earth or judge Him in His kingdom. How about when Jesus said to them that nothing by any means would harm them? Though all these things might have seemed impossible at first, little by little, they began to see the power of God activated through Christ, and their faith grew. They finally acknowledged that He was the Messiah and followed Him wholeheartedly.

No Answers!

As much as they attempted to understand this event, they couldn't. They examined it repeatedly, but all to no avail. When things can't be naturally explained, they must be spiritually discerned.

Have you ever been heartbroken and disappointed by an event, a person, or people? Many of us have been shattered by situations beyond our control and left with empty dreams, a blurred vision of the future, and confusion. I am so convinced that humans have been through this road.

The story mentioned above is very close to the hearts of all those who have been disappointed.

Human Reasoning!

For starters, let me say that the carnal mind is enmity to God. The carnal mind has its own set of beliefs and will never be supportive of God's idea, plan, or purpose. The flesh (the carnal mind) will pull us opposite from the Lord's purpose.

I'm not saying not to have any common sense, but nothing is more opposed to a walk of faith than the flesh and its ideas. Countless battles of the Spirit of God have been lost because the flesh won.

Once the servant of God is fully convinced that what God said must be thought through, challenged, and reasoned, God's will will be put off. Anything of the Lord will always have to fight against the flesh.

Jesus Sees Right Through Us!

As they walked home to Emmaus, Jesus appeared to them, but their eyes were restrained from recognizing Him. Jesus knew these followers were sad and thus asked them what was wrong. Why were they so downcast?

In response to this story, we will discover that they were sad because of all that had happened to Jesus and how it seemed that following Him was all for nothing.

When you and I don't know what we don't know, our reaction will be, for the most part, wrong and emotionally detrimental. We will falter unless we know the truth, which can only be understood in the inner man or the spirit of man. This happens to all.

Now, had their eyes been opened to see Jesus initially, their countenance would not have been sad. They would have been jumping for joy, full of expectation.

Don't Be Too Quick to Judge the External!

As I bring this devotion to a close, a great lesson to learn as we walk with God is never to assume that it is all lost just because the happy or joyful emotions are not there.

Sometimes, the Lord will have us exercise our faith by removing our natural abilities to understand or the ability to see how He sees.

It would be of great wisdom to us to see and then ask God, what is happening around me, in me, or through me, Lord? Always remember that the Lord is the only One who knows what is happening in us.

To be in such a place of disappointment and confusion is only an invitation to a deeper and more intimate walk with Jesus. Let us go after Him; He has all the answers we need! Neh'enah.

37

The Right!

"But as many as received Him, to them He gave the right to become children of God, to those who believe in His name: who were born, not of blood, nor of the will of the flesh, nor of the will of man, but of God." (John 1:12, 13)

When one comes to Christ by acknowledging their great need for a Savior, repenting of sin, and getting washed in the precious blood of Jesus, that man will find the heavy burden of sin to fall off him. In this, the man becomes a new creature in Christ (2 Corinthians 5:17).

This event will bring the lost sinner into God's kingdom, producing unspeakable joy and glory in their hearts. Yes, it is here where they will enjoy fellowship with God through the Holy Spirit. What a day this is!

How Can It Be Possible?

For many, this experience is nearly impossible. How can God forgive that sinful person? They ask. Why would God forgive them after all the wicked things they have committed? Then it becomes personal: How can God forgive me for all the sinful things I have done throughout my life? It is a good question; nevertheless, God does forgive and restore!

You see, a man can only come to Christ if he is willing to acknowledge his need for Christ. Every human being created will always fight to keep the driver's seat. He wants to drive and will not allow God to guide their lives. For humanity to relinquish the driver's seat is nearly impossible. The flesh demands to keep all rights! One can continue to falter and struggle through life, ignoring the invitations of the Holy Spirit until, one day, the truth of His word breaks in.

Once the individual acknowledges his need, he must yield his life and surrender ownership of his own life; it is here where a man allows God to take the driver's seat, and he willfully moves over. Yes, it is here where the man yields his right and picks up the right to become a child of God.

Do you see this?

Personal Rights!

A man is born in sin. It is not what he does that is sinful per se; it is what he is that disqualifies him from entering God's presence. The individual who doesn't know Christ personally is usually full of himself. He feels he is in control of his own life and thus lives how he wants to. Though this is a true statement, it doesn't help the individual's cause, for the man is in a sinful state and found short of the glory of God.

Living without Christ in this world is the epitome of selfishness. Man is full of himself and doesn't need God to lead him. As foolish as this belief may be, this is precisely what lost sinners go by.

When trying to talk to someone about the love of God for them or in attempting to point them to a life that is truly free in Christ, it usually ends up turning into an argument regarding religious preferences.

The lost man or woman will begin to justify their failures; they will quickly blame others for their misfortunes. Have you found this to be true in your witnessing of Christ?

Yielding Personal Rights

The yielding of personal rights is not only a hard thing to do but also impossible. A carnal person cannot find God by his merit. One cannot come to God alone, in his way, or by his desire. The Father must draw him. Jesus said, **"No one can come to Me unless the Father who sent Me draws him."**

When Invited to Come!

Once the Lord moves our hearts to come to Him, we must quickly accept the invite and, by faith, put our whole trust in Him. It is here where the magic happens in God!

The Scripture above says, **"But as many as received Him, to them He gave the right to become children of God..."** If the individual receives Christ's invitation into His life, a right is immediately given to become a child of God. So, one will yield their selfish rights and pick up God's right to become a new creature in Christ.

This godly right is the "ability to perform an action" to the extent that there are no hindrances in the way.

When the Lord invites us to enter, and we believe that we must do this, then by confessing with our hearts or mouths that He is Lord over us, we obtain the right to experience sonship. It is here where we become a child of God. This is the miracle of the new birth. This is the beginning of exercising your rights in God as His servant. Neh'enah.

38

Smitten by the Lord!

"And David's heart condemned him after he had numbered the people. So, David said to the LORD, "I have sinned greatly in what I have done; but now, I pray, O LORD, take away the iniquity of Your servant, for I have done very foolishly." (2 Samuel 24:10)

While in His presence, I came across this one powerful scene where David had just numbered Israel and took a census of the people. God incited David to do this and then called him out for it. Very strange.

In my meditation, I thought that sometimes God provokes something in us and waits to see how we react. If we do things that please Him, our spirit will feel peace, but if we do things that displease Him, we will experience deep conviction, as it was in David's life.

Scripture says that David's heart condemned him after he had numbered the people. The word condemned sounds harsh, but it simply means that David's heart was smitten, beaten, bothered, or all of these. David didn't feel good about doing the census because he knew God wasn't happy with it.

I don't know about you, but conviction and a hatred for sin are great things to possess. It only shows that you are alive to God and desire to please Him in every way, even though your flesh desires to do the opposite. This would describe a spiritual man in training.

Spiritual Training

In spiritual training, the servant of Christ must always deal with self. This is the first step to pleasing God. Luke 14:25-27 reads: **"Now great multitudes went with Him. And He turned and said to them, "If anyone comes to Me and does not hate his father and mother, wife and children, brothers, and sisters, yes, and his own life also, he cannot be My disciple. And whoever does not bear his cross and come after Me cannot be My disciple."**

We must see that self is the culprit, the obstacle, and the hindrance that will always fight against God's will in our lives. If you surrender your life to Christ and die to yourself by placing it on the cross, God's will can be practiced daily. If there is no death blow to the flesh, then practicing the presence of God becomes impossible!

Once a servant of Jesus knows what God expects from him, he will feel the burden of the Lord upon his own shoulders. People don't carry the burden of the Lord because they haven't died to self. They haven't felt what Jesus felt when He offered Himself as a ransom for many.

As David, a man after God's heart, was doing his best to please God and serve Him with full-hearted devotion, his heart was tested. God knew David. When God knows you well, He can trust you with anything. David was this man.

A True Confession Brings Repentance!

As soon as the Spirit of the Lord smote David in his innermost being, David confessed his sin before the Lord and said, **"I have sinned greatly in what I have done."** You see, unless one repents, there can't be any forgiveness. The first step to any restoration is true confession and repentance. Unless these things are in place, that man's future is in jeopardy.

To add to this confession, David said, **"...take away the iniquity of Your servant, for I have done very foolishly."** It doesn't get any clearer than this: David pleaded with God to erase the iniquity and admitted that he had done very foolishly. How many of us walk in this level of intimate confession before God?

I have discovered that the more intimate and accurate the confession, the easier the restoration becomes; the more thorough and specific the confession, the sweeter Jesus's embrace is!

A mentor of mine used to say that it is wise to write down

your sins as the Holy Spirit brings them to your remembrance. Write them down on paper and be as specific as possible. Then, begin to go down the line and confess every one of them as best as possible. He believed this type of confession would clear any guilt or shame the devil might save for a rainy day. I have practiced this to date.

In closing of these thoughts, being quick to confess and repent of sin is a key to freedom. The enemy often would have us ignore the conviction; at other times, the enemy would have us excuse it or justify it, but let me say that the real man or woman of God will be quick to admit and declare their foolishness. So, let us repent of the sin and be restored in God! Neh'enah.

39

Time for Renewal!

"But when he saw many of the Pharisees and Sadducees coming to his baptism, he said to them, "Brood of vipers! Who warned you to flee from the wrath to come? Therefore, bear fruits worthy of repentance, and do not think to say to yourselves, 'We have Abraham as our father.' For I say to you that God is able to raise up children to Abraham from these stones. And even now the ax is laid to the root of the trees. Therefore, every tree which does not bear good fruit is cut down and thrown into the fire. I indeed baptize you with water unto repentance, but He who is coming after me is mightier than I, whose sandals I am not worthy to carry. He will baptize you with the Holy Spirit and fire. His winnowing fan is in His hand, and He will thoroughly clean out His threshing floor, and gather His wheat into the barn; but He will burn up the chaff with unquenchable fire."** (Matthew 3:7-12)

Somehow, the Pharisees and Sadducees heard about John the Baptist, who had been baptizing people in the Jordan River. One day, they came to see what all the hype was about. John was ready for them as they made their way down by the river.

With a warm welcome, John said, **"Brood of vipers! What

warned you to flee from the wrath to come?

In other words, "Who invited you here?"

Clothed in Religion

"Therefore, bear fruits worthy of repentance, and do not think to say to yourselves, 'We have Abraham as our father.'"

As John dismantled the religious spirit that possessed these religious groups, he said, **"Bear fruits worthy of repentance...!"** It was John's way of saying, "Where is the faith that you claim in Jesus? You are not saved? You haven't changed from your religious ways!"

He further adds another issue: using their credentials as Abraham's children. Listen to this: **"... and do not think to say to yourselves, 'We have Abraham as our father.'** It was John's way of saying to them, "Don't use your paternal history to get you into the kingdom; it won't work!

These religious people were running around using their history as Hebrew children and the entitlement of being descendants from the lineage of Abraham.

God's Axe Is Here!

"And even now, the ax is laid to the tree's root. There-

fore, every tree which does not bear good fruit is cut down and thrown into the fire."

After laying down the excuses, it almost seems that John is saying, **"The time for playing religious games must stop. This is a new day, and the Lord is about to unleash His axe upon the fruitless. Any tree that doesn't bear fruit will be cut down and thrown into the fire!"**

As John continues to preach, he adds, **"I indeed baptize you with water unto repentance, but He who is coming after me is mightier than I, whose sandals I am not worthy to carry. He will baptize you with the Holy Spirit and fire."**

I believe John was attempting to say, "I only do the external stuff, like baptizing you in water. I can only point you the right way, but you must do it from the heart, or it won't count. I baptize you in water, but Jesus will baptize you in the Holy Spirit and fire."

The Spirit of Holiness

"His winnowing fan is in His hand, and He will thoroughly clean out His threshing floor, and gather His wheat into the barn; but He will burn up the chaff with unquenchable fire."

When a man or woman of God gets in touch with God,

one characteristic will be expressed – the baptism of fire! A spirit of burning begins to burn brightly and fiercely. It starts to consume all the works of the flesh. All the compromise, all the half-heartedness, all the selfishness, and God's wishes become the servant's wishes.

As I close this word, I want to challenge your heart to come before the Lord and make this your prayer for this year. Nothing less than a fresh touch of God will suffice in our living days. We need a touch of God to deal with the blackness of our darkness.

As a word of caution: If you are clinging to your past experiences, your past promises, your past prophesies, or if you are still holding on to the old move of God in your life and yet your life is no different, your ministry is at a standstill – it might be time for a fresh visitation of God to come upon your life! Neh'enah.

40

The Return of an Unclean Spirit Is a Test of Discipline!

"But when the unclean spirit has gone out of a man, it roams through dry [arid] places in search of rest, but it does not find any. Then it says, I will go back to my house from which I came out. And when it arrives, it finds the place unoccupied, swept, put in order, and decorated. Then it goes and brings with it seven other spirits more wicked than itself, and they go in and make their home there. And the last condition of that man becomes worse than the first. So also shall it be with this wicked generation." (Matthew 12:43-45 AMP)

One of the things that was in my heart this morning was this one set of Scriptures. It came to me in a dream last night, and I felt I needed to write what I believed the Holy Spirit was saying.

In my walk with the Lord, my attention and efforts to know God have always leaned toward knowing God intimately. The internal life of the Spirit has always fascinated me, and I tend to lend myself to things about a deeper life in God. Please hear my heart in this as I want to make sure you understand me when I share about the deeper life in God.

A Deeper Life

What do I mean when I speak of the deeper life in God? I am not referring to the ability to see ghosts, discern demon powers, or follow entities in my house or place of business. I believe this stuff exists, but when it comes to a deeper life in God, this stuff is truly irrelevant.

The deeper life in God has to do with one thing and one thing alone – the person of Jesus. Growing in holiness, understanding true brokenness, and why God shares His secrets with those who take the time to become intimate with Him.

A deeper life in God is more than attending prayer meetings, reading the Bible, or fasting occasionally. It has nothing to do with corporate church gatherings, concerts, or conferences. The deeper life is a disciplined life in which the servant of God lends himself fully (heart, mind, and spirit) to the will of God.

Most people who talk of being spiritual are not; most people who speak of maturing are not; and those who talk about spirits are probably more possessed than those who don't.

An Unclean Spirit Revisits an Empty House!

The Bible speaks of unclean spirits being cast out of people, and all this is true. However, the Scripture also talks about these same spirits returning to see what is happening with their former habitation. Check the conversation these spirits are having with themselves: **"Then it says, I will go back to my house from which I came out. And when it arrives, it finds the place unoccupied..."**

Follow me closely...

The word unoccupied suggests the house is empty and without a tenant. The Greek original text goes further. The word **scholazō** is unoccupied or empty, which means to be at leisure, hence, to devote oneself to.

When an individual gets delivered, a spirit or a demon leaves that man's mind. It will not contend with the authority of the Name of Jesus, so it leaves but will attempt to come back. Are spirits stupid? Not!

When the unclean spirit leaves, it will make a soon revisit. It is looking for a dry resting place [see Matthew 12:43]. It scopes out the house or the man's mind. He will evaluate the situation. If the mind of the man where it used to live is unoccupied or empty because the man is full of self and has been spending most of his life in leisure; if the man has been living for his pleasure and not God's, the unclean spirit will go and get seven other spirits that are more wicked than it. They will attempt to destroy that man once and for all the second time. Do you see this?

Full of God!

What is the heart of the matter?

The heart of the matter is that once a believer is delivered from evil forces or spirits, that man or woman must run and fall prostrate at Jesus' feet and align his or her heart and life with God's will. The Holy Spirit must fully occupy that man's heart so that nothing can allure or seduce him out of God's will.

The discipline needed here is to humble oneself under the mighty hand of God daily.

Don't let any days go by without meeting Jesus in the early morning for a season of prayer. We must always be conscious that the enemy of our souls will always be on the lookout for an empty house! Neh'enah.

41

Our Fellowship with Christ and the Father! – Part 1

"Then Jesus said to them, "Most assuredly, I say to you, unless you eat the flesh of the Son of Man and drink His blood, you have no life in you. Whoever eats My flesh and drinks My blood has eternal life, and I will raise him up on the last day. For My flesh is food indeed, and My blood is drink indeed. He who eats My flesh and drinks My blood abides in Me, and I in him." (John 6:53)

Waking up early this morning, I felt the Spirit of the Lord wanting me to share this truth regarding our fellowship with Christ and the Father. While meditating on the Scripture that I wrote above, I was also quickened by the subject of God's life. If we have entered Christ, we will have life! If we have not entered Christ, then we don't have life. We must realize this and the impact this truth has on our destiny.

Everything we are and ever hope to be as Christ's followers will depend upon our fellowship with Christ and the Father. To the degree that we know God is to the degree that our destiny becomes brighter to the glory of God.

Let me share some thoughts that came to my heart as I

prayed this morning regarding this fellowship with God.

The Blood is Life!

For starters, let me say that one of the most valuable teachings in the Bible is the teaching of the blood sacrifice. Every sacrifice made to the Lord required that an animal die. In other words, blood was needed to complete the sacrifice. An animal had to die, and its blood was to be sprinkled before the altar. This was Old Testament protocol.

On the day of atonement, the high priest couldn't present himself before God without blood. He had to bring blood with him before he could enter the Holy of Holies. According to Leviticus 16, he was commanded to sprinkle blood upon the mercy seat. The blood provided access to God's presence.

In the same way today, without the blood of Jesus, we can't come into God's presence; without the blood of Jesus, we have no access and thus no life! But thanks be to God for Jesus our Lord, who paid the total price by dying and shedding blood on the cross of Calvary!

The Blood Has Brought Us Near!

"But now in Christ Jesus, you who once were far off have been brought near by the blood of Christ." (Ephesians 2:13)

Because of the shed blood, you and I can access the Father and fellowship with God. This is one of the greatest miracles we can experience as we come to the Lord in humility and a surrendered life.

As we are covered in His blood, not only are our sins covered and taken away, but our future finds purpose as we discover real life.

This Life is Contingent!

"But if we walk in the light as He is in the light, we have fellowship with one another, and the blood of Jesus Christ His Son cleanses us from all sin." (1 John 1:7)

For this life to be operative in us, we must be willing to walk in the light as He (Jesus) is in the light. The benefits of an extraordinary life in God are contingent upon our practice of walking in the light.

To have fellowship with Jesus and the Father, one must align themselves with God's divine order and walk in the light. If we walk in the light, then the blood of Jesus will operate in us and cleanse us from all sin. This is a progressive work.

So long as we are in fellowship with God, the blood will cleanse and keep us in fellowship; if we decide that we don't want this fellowship, we get ourselves out of God's will and flow of cleansing. At this point, we begin to get weak and weary.

Most of our failures in our walk with God are due to our inability to decide who we will follow – Jesus or the flesh. So, we battle to make this decision repeatedly. We have all been here.

We must be willing to please God with our whole hearts and minds. Listen to the first of the two great commandments: **"'You shall love the Lord your God with all your heart, soul, and mind."**

Please note how it calls us to give all of ourselves- not just one-fourth or one-half, but all, all, all! All our hearts, all our souls, and all our minds. Neh'enah.

42

Our Fellowship with Christ and the Father! – Part 2

While continuing this message of having fellowship with Christ and the Father, we must know that all our lives are wrapped up in this fellowship with God.

Also, know that the blood of Jesus has opened the way for you and me to discover God's extraordinary destiny. It is His eternal plan for all of us who believe.

This brings me to the following valuable lesson in this fellowship with God: how we often affect our futures by not allowing God to lead us in the way.

Let me take you to that lonely and challenging night for Jesus in the garden of Gethsemane.

The Spirit Is Willing; the Flesh is Weak!

There was this event at this garden called Gethsemane that took place right before Christ was to be arrested and taken in to be judged and then horribly crucified. It was a critical moment in the life of Christ and the life of the disciples. Listen to this:

"He went a little farther and fell on His face, and prayed, saying, "O My Father, if it is possible, let this cup pass from Me; nevertheless, not as I will, but as You will." Then He came to the disciples, found them sleeping, and said to Peter, "What! Could you not watch with Me for one hour? Watch and pray, lest you enter into temptation. The spirit indeed is willing, but the flesh is weak." (Matthew 26:39-41)

If there was ever a time when the disciples needed to step out and do what they felt in their hearts, it was this night. When Jesus needed their moral support, the disciples couldn't even help themselves.

The battle within them went on through the night until Christ was arrested. Let us examine this closely.

Jesus said that the spirit was willing. This means that the spirit within wanted God's desires to please God with all its strength; however, the flesh also had the same intensified desire. It tried to please self. This is the battle that you and I face daily. Sometimes, the struggle is more intense than others, but we all have these intensified battles to overcome the flesh.

It was Jesus' way of saying that you have a battle within and must choose who you will obey!

These servants of God were overcome or overtaken by

their flesh and fell asleep. Did they love Jesus? I believe they did. Did they want to obey Jesus? I think that they did. Then why did they fall asleep? My friends, to be just, let's say that this has happened to all of us. We have all yielded to our lower nature, to our flesh, and have failed. It was all due to a weak spirit!

If this were the only thing that happened to us, we could repent and say to God, "Maybe, next time, I'll get it right, God!" And move on. But this is not all that happens. It is way more severe than we think. I'll show you.

Lukewarmness!

There is a sickness or disease worse than COVID-19 or cancer. It is called lukewarmness. Lukewarmness is not a state of being - lukewarmness is a disease that believers develop by living an undecided, self-absorbed, rebellious life. They can't decide who to follow. Listen to what James says about people who can't believe God: **"If any of you lacks wisdom, let him ask God, who gives generously to all without reproach, and it will be given him. But let him ask in faith, with no doubting, for the one who doubts is like a wave of the sea that is driven and tossed by the wind. For that person must not suppose that he will receive anything from the Lord; he is a double-minded man, unstable in all his ways."** (James 1:5-8)

Let me continue to illustrate:

"And to the angel of the church of the Laodiceans write, 'These things says the Amen, the Faithful and True Witness, the Beginning of the creation of God: "I know your works, that you are neither cold nor hot. I could wish you were cold or hot. So then, because you are lukewarm, and neither cold nor hot, I will vomit you out of My mouth. Because you say, 'I am rich, have become wealthy, and have need of nothing'—and do not know that you are wretched, miserable, poor, blind, and naked...". (Revelation 3:14-17)

God knows something about us that no one knows. It says that he knows our works, that we are neither cold nor hot. He makes his wish known and says, **" I wish you were one or the other. " He further adds, " Because you are lukewarm, I will vomit you out of my mouth. "**

Here's how people try to cover up their lukewarmness: They say, I am rich, have become wealthy, and need nothing. But God knows the truth and says, you are wretched, miserable, poor, blind, and naked.

You see, God knows us very well. People know us, but not like God knows us. We all face this battle for destiny, God's purpose, eternal values, etc.

Let Us Return to Our First Love!

As we battle to align ourselves back to the Lord, repentance is crucial for our return. Unless we acknowledge that we have missed God's wishes, we won't have anything to repent of. Too often, this seems to be the case. People don't think they have done anything wrong!

Let me say that as one humbles themselves under the mighty hand of God, that servant will realize that they have missed God. That conviction hits us at this place, and we can decide to repent and follow hard after God.

Let us recognize where we stand and make some changes in our mindset. We will have a lukewarm heart unless we learn to discern and decide God's wishes. We already know the end to this. Neh'enah.

43

The Benefit of Strife and Contention!

"Lot also, who went with Abram, had flocks and herds and tents. Now the land was not able to support them, that they might dwell together, for their possessions were so great that they could not dwell together. And there was strife between the herdsmen of Abram's livestock and the herdsmen of Lot's livestock. The Canaanites and the Perizzites then dwelt in the land. So Abram said to Lot, "Please let there be no strife between you and me, and between my herdsmen and your herdsmen; for we are brethren. Is not the whole land before you? Please separate from me. If you take the left, then I will go to the right; or, if you go to the right, then I will go to the left." (Genesis 13:5-9)

I find something hidden regarding God's counsel in the passages I will share with you. The Lord always uses daily life situations to teach us His heart. We must never forget that God's ways are not our ways!

Mysteries of Life

I don't know why we sometimes face things beyond our understanding, questionable and mysterious. For example, when God puts people together so they can work on a specific project, and they end up getting angry at one another for no particular reason, I don't get this.

In the abovementioned story, Abram leaves his land and brings his nephew Lot. I don't know the purpose of this, but there might be a critical point. As they traveled together, they both became very prosperous; they were so prosperous that they could not fit in the lot of land that they had. This causes strife among the herdsmen, which prompts Abram to separate from his nephew Lot.

Is there a Solution to the Problem?

Is this one of those times when we ask ourselves, "Is this God's way of separating these two entities for a greater purpose? " Or do we work it out with the other party and don't part ways but come to an agreement?

How do we know what God is doing in these situations? Let us look a bit further.

Here's my take on all of this...

Contentions and Disagreements Anyone?

Disagreement among people, groups, leaders, etc., is a sign that change must occur. Yes, but what kind of change?

If you are a spiritual father, you want the best for all parties involved. There must be a detachment before any significant change can occur. A spiritual father will desire maturity and growth in all parties involved. A selfish person will not care about others but only their own. Always notice this.

When dealing with a selfish leader, you will always get into strife. This strife is an immature characteristic. Usually, one person sees the future, while another only sees the present. Which one are you?

Separations must occur, but the real challenge is how to do it peacefully.

Let us take the story of Paul and Barnabas as another example of this:

Paul's View of John Mark

"Then, after some days, Paul said to Barnabas, "Let us now go back and visit our brethren in every city where we have preached the word of the Lord and see how they are doing." Now Barnabas was determined to take with them John called Mark. But Paul insisted that they should not take with them the one who had departed from them in Pamphylia and had not gone with them to the work. Then the contention became so sharp that they parted from one another. And so, Barnabas took Mark and sailed to Cyprus; but Paul chose Silas and departed,

being commended by the brethren to the grace of God. And he went through Syria and Cilicia, strengthening the churches." (Acts 15:36-41)

The Scripture tells us the story of this strong contention between Paul and Barnabas regarding the younger John Mark. Was it of the Lord that Paul and Barnabas would part ways? We will never know, but what we do know is that the gospel, in turn, went further because of this.

Sometimes, God must make changes in our midst that cause us to question why He has allowed certain things. I have experienced some of this in my journey with God and ministry.

Despite how I feel about something, God does what He needs to do. I do plan, but God orders all my steps. My heart desires to be an excellent spiritual father and mentor to those under my leadership.

May we all grow in the likeness of Christ and do all He has asked us to do here on earth. Neh'enah.

44

The Calling!

"And when He had called His twelve disciples to Him, He gave them power over unclean spirits, to cast them out, and to heal all kinds of sickness and all kinds of disease. Now the names of the twelve apostles are these: first, Simon, who is called Peter, and Andrew his brother; James the son of Zebedee, and John his brother; Philip and Bartholomew; Thomas and Matthew the tax collector; James the son of Alphaeus, and Lebbaeus, whose surname was Thaddaeus; Simon the Canaanite, and Judas Iscariot, who also betrayed Him." (Matthew 10:1-4)

While in prayer this early morning, I came across this passage of Scripture that lays out some essential facts concerning the man God uses. I could discern what God has called them to do regarding priority, what type of ministry work to do, and the choices they will make when following Christ.

As the Spirit of revelation opened my heart, I saw how Jesus first called His twelve disciples to Himself.

The calling begins with getting to know Christ. One must learn to draw near to His heart and mind; the servant must understand that He can be thoroughly equipped for every good work only as He allows himself to be taught by God. Now, this He had called His twelve disciples to Him speaks to me of an invitation to a more intimate life with Christ. The Spirit invites us to draw near, be with Him, and learn His ways. Often, believers think that salvation is the beginning and the end of a new life; my friends, it is only the beginning of a journey into the unknown.

In Colossians 1:18, the Scriptures say that Christ is the head of the body, the church. This means He directs us how to go, and this is always! He leads His people personally, locally, and globally. He is our Leader, and yes, He can be trusted.

Intimacy

The ministry of the Lord begins with an invitation to an intimate walk with Him. This is the pattern. People think doing works for Christ is the key to walking with God; I beg to differ. The call begins with a willingness to surrender ALL to Jesus. It's a call to be with Him and be at His feet as a lifestyle, not only when we hit a crossroads.

We won't understand God's design until we become God's errand boys!

The life of intimacy is perhaps the life most believers don't understand. It is not appealing to the flesh, but it is to God. To surrender and fully yield to the voice and direction of God is not for someone filled with his ambitions. Intimacy with God is rarely attained by the "selfish!" It is a fight to serve God or please the flesh. No wonder most people don't bother with prayer and developing an intimate life with God.

The Work of Ministry

Serving Jesus is being Christ to the broken, needy, and captive. Ministry is an expression of God's love to those in need. The servant of God must be conscious first of the spiritual life of the people he is ministering to. Without a ministry toward the spiritual and soulish part of humanity, it becomes a social service, not a spiritual one.

When the Scripture says that Christ gave them power over unclean spirits, cast them out, and healed all kinds of sickness and all kinds of disease, it means that God had empowered His servants to do what He was already doing. He desired that His servants would be an extension of His grace to the people long after He would be gone.

Ministry to the lost [those without Christ in their hearts, those in bondage to sin, sickness, and many other vices] is an expression of what God has deposited inside all His servants.

After a servant of Christ has been in God's presence and intimacy with God, the Spirit of the Lord will download the strategy of ministering to the needy by using the servant's talents, abilities, giftings, etc. All forms of ministry must begin in the secret place of prayer first!

Choices!

Revelation always gives birth to desire deep within the human heart. This desire is like a fire embedded into the human heart and mind. After a time, the desire begins to wane if not attended to. It is like a voice crying out in the wilderness, longing to be heard.

Now, desire without discipline is like wanting to go from one side of a river to another but don't have a bridge to cross.

Attaining desire is more challenging than someone might think. Still, discipline is even more complex because it involves consistent action and practice of what one believes to be instrumental to getting a desired end.

Visions, dreams, prophetic words, and promises are all excellent for instilling desire and passion; yet, if action is not followed through, if discipline is not used to make the desire come to pass, it is all for naught!

Always remember that following Christ will be a dogfight. You must want Christ's will badly for it to affect you fully. Intimacy will breed ministry; after this, choices must be made. We get to choose. Neh'enah.

45

Discerning the Wicked and Their Mindset!

**"For the wicked boasts of his heart's desire;
He blesses the greedy and renounces the LORD.
The wicked in his proud countenance does not seek God;
God is in none of his thoughts."** (Psalm 10:3, 4)

In meditating on these few verses, the Spirit of the Lord revealed this to me, which I would like to share with you.

Many people claim allegiance to Christ but do it only with lip service. They don't love Jesus from the heart. Am I a judge to my brother or sister who says that they love Jesus but don't? Of course, I am not a judge.

My calling is to edify His church from the foundation up to maturity. I also call on others to align their lives so that their futures will be pleasing to the Lord. This is possible only by faith and God's grace.

In my work of establishing the believers in their relationship with God, many things must be at work simultaneously. For example, we must know that man comprises three parts: spirit, soul, and body. These three parts must be aligned with God's purpose.

Man's change or transformation begins in the spirit, in his inner being, where the Spirit of God mingles with his human spirit. At this level, man receives revelation from God through the Spirit of God into his human spirit, which animates it to respond in a godly way. This is a willful choice.

Secondly, his soul processes the spiritual information and is called to yield or fight against it. If you are born again, the Spirit of the Lord will raise a standard against your flesh so that you may please God with your actions.

If the person has not received Christ into their hearts, then the soulish part of him will only do what the flesh desires, which is everything God is against. It is not about carrying a good deed that pleases God; it has never been about good works. It is about allowing Christ to have the preeminence in our lives. This is what pleases the Lord.

The body will do what it is told to do by the Spirit of God or the flesh.

If you are walking with the Lord, choose who you will please.

In discerning who pleases God and who walks in wickedness, we must look deeper and way beyond the good works; we must look into a man's heart.

The Wicked

Psalm 10 speaks to us about the wicked. Who are the wicked? Who are these people whom the Psalmist calls out as boasters?

The wicked are the opposite of godly people. They dwell on the idea of being evil. Their intentions are always to do wrong or harm. Wickedness and godlessness are characteristics that dress a man in evil attire. This is found in the old nature, that sensual part of every human being. We all have the potential to be this.

The Psalmist says the wicked boasts of his heart's desire. In discerning wicked people, they will always boast of their own heart's desires. Not God's!

Wicked people tend to give themselves away by always boasting about how great their ideas are. Have you ever noticed some evil people around you?

Another critical thing to notice or discern in wicked people is that he [the wicked] blesses the greedy and renounces the LORD. Isn't it strange that greedy people only hang around with greedy people? Typically, a greedy man attracts another greedy person without fail. I have seen this through the years. Only greedy people sympathize with greedy people. Notice also how the wicked don't mind the Lord but renounce Him. They despise or treat the Lord with contempt. Total wickedness in action!

Another thing to discern in a wicked person is that he practices daily; the wicked, in his proud countenance, does not seek God. The evil person always feels comfortable in his self and feels no need to seek God. The greatest of all failures is for man to think he is complete and does not need his Creator. Too many have walked this road only to discover the painful end.

Finally, as we walk among people, the wicked will always be known for their lack of knowledge of God. The Scripture says, **"God is in none of his** [the wicked] **thoughts."** The wicked don't want anyone altering their lifestyle, so they keep the Lord out of their thoughts. They live for themselves and only to please themselves. They will destroy anyone who comes close to them, for they are like a raging fire of selfishness.

As I close this meditation, learn to discern the wicked in your midst. You will be wise to do so. Neh'enah.

46

Overcoming Earthly Attachments! – Part 1

"Whoever does not carry his own cross [expressing a willingness to endure whatever may come] **and follow after Me** [believing in Me, conforming to My example in living and, if need be, suffering or perhaps dying because of faith in Me] **cannot be My disciple."** (Luke 14:27. Amplified Version)

This morning, while I met with the Lord for prayer, my heart was quickened by this reality: We can only go as far as the length of the cord!

In my vision of God this morning, the Lord showed me an individual tied to a tree by a cord about 15 feet long. As he attempted to walk away from the tree, he would only go as far as the cord would let him. The Spirit caused me to see the tree as an earthly attachment and the cord as our personal will. To the degree that we are willing to break this cord off, we will be free to give God more of us!

Earthly attachments are things that counter God's will. They can be material, emotional, physical, or mental obstructions. For fear of not understanding, we abort the possibility of entering a greater fullness of Christ.

Cords Are Arguments in the Mind Against God's Knowledge.

"For the weapons of our warfare are not physical [weapons of flesh and blood], but they are mighty before God for the overthrow and destruction of strongholds, [Inasmuch as we] refute arguments and theories and reasonings and every proud and lofty thing that sets itself up against the [true] knowledge of God; and we lead every thought and purpose away captive into the obedience of Christ (the Messiah, the Anointed One)." (2 Corinthians 10:4, 5 Amplified Version)

The arguments we make that hide behind these self-made fortresses (strongholds) have been the culprits in our stagnation. Fear, doubt, preconceived ideas, and lack of faith have all contributed to our missing the most fantastic hour yet.

What About the Eleven?

"And in the fourth watch [between 3:00–6:00 a.m.] of the night, Jesus came to them, walking on the sea. And when the disciples saw Him walking on the sea, they were terrified and said, It is a ghost! And they screamed out with fright. But instantly, He spoke to them, saying, Take courage! I AM! Stop being afraid! And Peter answered Him, Lord, if it is You, command me to come to You on the water. He said, Come! So Peter got out of

the boat and walked on the water, and he came toward Jesus." (Matthew 14:25-29)

They saw a ghost walking on the water. One of the hindrances that those who would and should advance in God is failing to recognize Jesus coming to us in a different form. We know it wasn't a ghost walking on water but Jesus Himself.

Our fleshly perception of Christianity must be altered and elevated to where Jesus is. It is time to leave old structures, systems, and perceptions of who and how God works in our lives today. Let him who has an ear hear!

"But instantly, He spoke to them, saying, Take courage! I AM! Stop being afraid!" The Lord's mercy has kept us flowing in Him; if not for His mercy, none of us would be here today. Knowing that the disciples got scared, He unveiled Himself and said, I AM!

What Will the Disciples Do Next?

Jesus unveiled Himself to them and allowed them to taste the life to come, yet their minds insisted on past experiences. Many have attempted to bring God back to our level of comprehension. We must recognize what God is doing in us and walk in it!

"And Peter answered Him, Lord if it is You, command

me to come to You on the water. He said, Come!"

This verse teaches us about Peter in a way that other Scriptures don't. We see Peter talking to Jesus amid this experience, saying, **"Lord, if it is You, command me to come to You on the water."** Unlike the other eleven disciples on the boat, Peter didn't deal with the argument of fear but of doubt. Yet amid His doubt, He made a request and said, **"...command me to come to You!"**

The difference between Peter and the other eleven disciples was that Peter didn't allow the cord of fear to hold him down from entering a higher level of God's destiny for Him. This is why Jesus responded to Peter and said, **"Come."** He didn't stay in the boat; He walked on water!

Still on the Boat?!

As Peter walked on the water, the other eleven never even considered taking a plunge into the deep! They probably praised Peter, cheered for Peter, clapped for Peter, and encouraged Peter, but that is as far as it went; this sounds like much of what we see in those who pledge allegiance to Christ today. Too many arguments come from our self-made strongholds, propagating fear and doubt concerning the will of God for our lives.

Consequently, our fears and doubts keep our lives from entering God's plan. We convince ourselves that it's not

God's timing, plan, intention, or will for us; yes, all because of fear and doubt in our minds and hearts.

As I close this meditation, consider your life and all God longs to accomplish in and through you. Learn to recognize God in the Spirit, not in form, or we might miss His visitation. Neh'enah.

47

Overcoming Earthly Attachments! – Part 2

"Do not love or cherish the world or the things that are in the world. If anyone loves the world, love for the Father is not in him. For all that is in the world—**the lust of the flesh** [craving for sensual gratification] **and the lust of the eyes** [greedy longings of the mind], **and the pride of life** [assurance in one's own resources or in the stability of earthly things]—**these do not come from the Father but are from the world** [itself]. **And the world passes away and disappears, and with it the forbidden cravings (the passionate desires, the lust) of it; but he who does the will of God and carries out His purposes in his life abides (remains) forever."** (1 John 2:15-17 Amplified Version)

In our attempt to please God and walk uprightly in His ways, we must be intentional about the steps we take by faith. We can't expect to be pleasing to the Lord when earthly attachments possess our hearts and minds. Isn't it no wonder that too many so-called believers today leave Bible-led churches and ministries in exchange for the hyperbole of religious meetings without the presence of God?

In John's words, he says, **"Do not love or cherish the world or the things that are in the world."** He adds, **"If anyone**

loves the world, love for the Father is not in him."

In plain English, John is telling the followers of Jesus that the world is a system that is coming down; don't be enslaved by it, don't invest in it, and don't be led away by its seduction.

In saying this, allow me to continue building on the revelation I shared on *Overcoming Earthly Attachments – Part 1*.

Earthly attachments are obstacles in our pursuit of Christ. They come to us very subtly and with a clear intention to draw us away from loving God with all we have: our hearts and minds, our emotions, our time, our finances, and our giftings, to list a few.

Let us look at a few cords that can either oppress us or bless us . . .

Cords that We Have Created Ourselves.

Cords that we create ourselves are all too familiar. These cords attach us to our emotions, doubts, fears, how we think, process, and conclude, and yes, even how we think about our future.

Too many believers today are bound to their belief system because they are too afraid to take a risk in the Lord. Their mindset is filled with failure and its possibilities. The past binds them. Too much pain or trauma has left them sidelined. I believe that a man or woman who has experienced such things can come to the Lord and, by the power of His blood, be restored afresh and become a valuable vessel for Jesus.

Cords that Others Have Created in Us

In other forms of bondage, some have allowed other people to manipulate and control them. Fear of man is usually another cord that keeps God's servants from pleasing the Lord. People involved in toxic relationships must consider what God thinks about them. People who are married and are unequally yoked with unbelievers – follow the chain of command and do the will of God. Unless the husband is beating the wife up and is violent, that woman must stay and fight for her husband's soul till he comes to Christ. This is not an easy thing; yet, if a mistake was made in marrying such a one, this may be the price of learning a great lesson.

Cords that the Lord Has Made for Us

Part of our walk with the Lord involves recognizing the sphere of influence God has placed us in. While some might want to do exciting and outwardly promising things, consider what God thinks about them first. This is wisdom.

People tend to get excited about worldly or fleshly ideas so quickly. It almost seems that they can't wait for the latest fad to come out so they can participate in it.

Too often, believers end up in such harsh situations because of their foolishness—no one else's! They are presumptuous and move in so-called faith, only to discover that it wasn't God after all. This can be excruciating.

If we allow ourselves to follow God's leadership—in it—we will find a cord of love. He will cover those led by Him and purposely walk in the sphere He has placed them in.

Earthly attachments are the greatest hindrances to any believer in the United States.

We must embrace Christ's cross and pursue God's heart with all our strength to overcome this spiritual sickness. The cost doesn't matter; we live or die based on our embrace of Jesus our Lord. Neh'enah.

48

Will You Sin Against God? Character Test 1

"Now Joseph was handsome in form and appearance. And it came to pass after these things that his master's wife cast longing eyes on Joseph, and she said, "Lie with me." But he refused and said to his master's wife, "Look, my master does not know what is with me in the house, and he has committed all that he has to my hand. There is no one greater in this house than I, nor has he kept back anything from me but you, because you are his wife. How then can I do this great wickedness, and sin against God?" (Genesis 39:6-9)

When I read these verses early this morning, I heard the Spirit within me ask, "Will you follow God or your selfish desires?" At first, these words sound so simple and almost comical that God would ask that of someone. You would think that is a given. Yet, the Spirit knows all things and will quicken our hearts; plus, there is a reason why God enlightens our hearts with His truth.

Further reading this powerful life lesson, I thought Joseph was being tested on character. No matter where in the Scriptures you read, our character will constantly be tested and under probation. One man said, "We are under probation twenty-four hours a day for the rest of our lives."

I believe God is always working in us so that He may work through us. We are constantly being broken and built up in our most holy faith. The Lord intends to allow us to experience some challenging character-building exercises. We must all be tested.

The Importance of Character

Character is like the foundation of a building. If the foundation is strong, it will hold whatever you build on it. The structure won't be held up if the foundation is weak, and the loss will be significant. So, yes, God will work on the foundation of our souls and character.

What is character? One man defines it as the person you really are when no one is looking. This definition or explanation should clarify it for all of us.

Joseph Recognized the Potential Wickedness

A critical part of developing a godly character is recognizing when one is about to be tested and enter great danger. When we realize what we are against, we must hear the Lord and move as fast and far away from danger.

Any individual might think that anyone can do that, but I beg to differ. Moving away from potential danger when everything inside you doesn't want to is not an easy challenge for anyone.

You and I have had our challenges in character development. Many battles have come and gone, and some can say, "I have conquered them all!" Others may say, "I was tested and failed, but I'm up and going again!"

No one is exempt from being tested by the Lord for the sole purpose of character development. We will all drink from this cup as Christ forms in us. If you love Jesus, be ready for this.

When Potiphar's wife approached Joseph with lust in her heart, she wasn't doing anything out of the ordinary. She was probably a lonely woman and was possessed by lust. We can't say very much about her history, but we know Potiphar's wife had inclinations towards unfaithfulness. She was the tool that God used to test Joseph's faithfulness.

Faithfulness to the Lord!

"How then can I do this great wickedness and sin against God?"

Joseph's first call was to Jehovah God. Joseph was faithful to the Lord and didn't want to disappoint His heart. He was a God-possessed man! Potiphar's wife was an ungodly woman with a natural desire to forsake everything essential or valuable.

The test will always be on God's vessel. He will be the one tested, not the other person. He who thinks he or she has God's touch will always be in God's mind as tests come his or her way.

What Kept Joseph from Sin?

With conviction in my heart, I believe Joseph was kept from sinning with Potiphar's wife due to his humble devotion to God. Our dedication will constantly be tested. We must know this. If you are ever tested in your character, always ask yourself this: Am I devoted to Christ?

Our devotion to Christ is created in the secret place of prayer. Show me a man who is out of touch with God due to the lack of personal communion and prayer, and I'll show you a man full of compromising rebellion and sin.

We must return to the throne room, and once there, shut the world out and allow your heart to melt in Jesus' loving arms as you cry out for mercy and a fresh touch of His holiness! Neh'enah.

49

Will You Sin Against God? Character Test 2

"And the king was sorry; nevertheless, because of the oaths and because of those who sat with him, he commanded it to be given to her. So, he sent and had John beheaded in prison. And his head was brought on a platter and given to the girl, and she brought it to her mother. Then his disciples came and took away the body and buried it and went and told Jesus." (Matthew 14:9-12)

I want to continue the excellent character development challenge as we open Matthew 14:9-12. Let me ask: When under pressure, will you fear God or man? Will you act on behalf of the Lord, or will you please your flesh?

One issue with those who claim such allegiance to Christ is that they tend to aggrandize their faith. These servants tend to be vocal about their devotion to Christ; however, when it comes to character development, they fall short of what their words say.

One thing I have learned about character development is that its formation is deep, and it takes time to develop according to God's pattern. In short, let me just put it out there and say it is not easy being a disciple of Jesus, not so much because of the outward critics but the inward challenges of transformation in the likeness of Christ!

This is one reason the test of character is lonely, long, and extremely painful. Yet the Lord calls us to such a life.

Enslaved by Your Own Words!

**"My child, if you have put up security for a friend's debt or agreed to guarantee the debt of a stranger—
if you have trapped yourself by your agreement
and are caught by what you said—
follow my advice and save yourself,
for you have placed yourself at your friend's mercy."**
(Proverbs 6:1-3)

In the abovementioned story, as found in Matthew 14:9-12, I learned a few principles in this scene. Allow me to share.

King Herod happened to be celebrating his birthday and was being warned by John the Baptist that it was wrong to have his brother's wife put John in prison. Now, the king was fearful of John the Baptist. He did respect him as a prophet and didn't want to kill him, at least not initially.

Once the celebration started, Heredia's daughter danced before the King and enslaved his mind and heart. This young lady pleased Herod to the point that Herod was mesmerized by her and promised with an oath to give her whatever she might ask.

As a lesson to be learned from history, this King got in a very compromising position and fell into a trap due to his stupor. For one, the King made many promises and oaths to someone he was lusting after. Herein lies the mistake of too many servants of God: We buy into a godless idea and become servants of it!

One should always be careful not to fall into the enemy's trap and enslave or ensnare themselves by other people—not in the name of friendship or politics. The end may be consequential.

The Scripture in Matthew 14 says, "**...Because of the oaths and because of those who sat with him... he commanded it [John's head] to be given to her**".

In walking with Jesus, we will be challenged. There will be people who will try to trap us with their words, their acts of kindness towards us, etc. All in the name of buying us, enslaving us, or ensnaring us. We must be watchful.

When we follow the will of the Lord too many times, we look for a convenient way to do things for God. Instead of following the process of the Lord, we begin to look for people with "cloud." Yes, those people with high positions, who are famous and who everyone seems to listen to.

The flesh always wants to take a shortcut and undermine

the process of God. This is all too common in our day. It was common in ancient days and is probably even more today!

We tend to facilitate our process by going to these folks and subtly getting under their "cloud" of influence. Is this the Lord's will for a real man of God? I think not! The Lord may allow us to meet someone with influence to propagate the gospel, but note that God's way must be done, not man's way!

Remember the inviting voice that will challenge your leadership as I close this devotion.

The Lord sometimes brings people into our lives with selfish desires only to test our hearts. The Lord wants to know what is really in our hearts. It takes a real man or woman of God to wait upon the Lord. Consider this. Neh'enah.

50

The Appreciation of Crumbs!

"Then Jesus went out from there and departed to the region of Tyre and Sidon. And behold, a woman of Canaan came from that region and cried out to Him, saying, "Have mercy on me, O Lord, Son of David! My daughter is severely demon-possessed." But He answered her not a word. And His disciples came and urged Him, saying, "Send her away, for she cries out after us." But He answered and said, "I was not sent except to the lost sheep of the house of Israel." Then she came and worshiped Him, saying, "Lord, help me!" But He answered and said, "It is not good to take the children's bread and throw it to the little dogs." And she said, "Yes, Lord, yet even the little dogs eat the crumbs which fall from their masters' table." Then Jesus answered and said to her, "O woman, great is your faith! Let it be to you as you desire." And her daughter was healed from that very hour." (Matthew 15:21-28)

The first thing that came to my mind as I pondered these verses was, how dare she come to Jesus and make demands on Him? Doesn't she know, has she not been informed, that Jesus came to touch the lost sheep of the house of Israel? The answer is we don't know. Even if she knew this to be accurate, I genuinely believe she would still have come to talk to Jesus about her demon-possessed daughter.

Not a Word!

After the woman makes her need known to Jesus, the Scripture says, **"He answered her not a word."** Why do you suppose He didn't comment? While Jesus pondered the depth of her heart cry, the disciples had another idea, {they} came and urged Him, saying, **"Send her away, for she cries out after us."**

In thinking deeply about this matter, we must know that God always listens to the cries of those who make their request known out of a broken heart. Not answering when we want Him to does not signify that He isn't going to do something about our request. This thought must always be before us.

Now, as for the outside forces, this is a different story. The fleshly urgency to walk away from a potential breakthrough in our lives is always present. People surround our lives who don't have our best interests in mind; voices deep within our hearts challenge our faith, our requests, and our perseverance. We must stay before God until He answers yes or no!

While Jesus ponders every word this woman speaks to Him, I can only imagine the Lord squeezing out the honey of this woman's faith. Her need is real, and her situation is becoming more and more detrimental daily; this woman needs a breakthrough!

It Must Go Deeper!

Let me say that even with all our needs, tears, and moans, the Lord is not moved to act. He is looking for something more than just an external want; He is looking for an internal expression of brokenness. He is looking for someone willing to lay it all down for the sake of others! The request must go deeper.

The disciples had already written this lady off. They were not discerning of her words; they were not concerned with her need, especially since she was from the region of Tyre and Sidon. **"Send her away,"** they said to Jesus.

Then Jesus spoke!

"I was not sent except to the lost sheep of the house of Israel."

I'm Not Going Away!

The woman pleaded and **"came and worshiped Him, saying, "Lord, help me!"**

Can you picture this event in the life of Jesus' ministry? He couldn't get rid of this woman. He couldn't chase her off! No one could take her away from this holy moment. Finally, Jesus told her the truth: **"It is not good to take the children's bread and throw it to the little dogs."**

Jesus likened her to a little dog!

One would think, OK, Jesus, I get it! You are God, and I'm just a loser! It's OK, Jesus; I will go about my business and never bother you again! But she didn't think of doing this. The woman stayed before Him and pressed in, for her request had yet to be answered.

The woman replied to Jesus' words, saying, **"Yes, Lord, yet even the little dogs eat the crumbs that fall from their masters' table."** Amazing!

We see the woman's reply coming from the depth of her soul, saying, You see, Lord, even if you call me a dog, I will eat whatever comes from the table. Leftovers, crumbs, anything. It's ok. My need is much greater, and only you can help me. So call me what you want, but I'm not going away until my request is met!

Faith Has No Limits!

"Then Jesus answered and said to her, "O woman, great is your faith! Let it be to you as you desire." And her daughter was healed from that very hour."

It wasn't her words, tears, or cry before Jesus that moved Him; it was her faith screaming to be heard. It was her faith crossing every obstacle known to man. She knew who He was, and Jesus knew who she was! She was a woman with a specific faith He was well acquainted with—the faith of God!

In closing, let the Spirit of God teach you to pray according to the power of God's faith (not your human faith). If you allow the Spirit to touch your spirit, you will always please God and move His hand! Neh'enah.

51

Learning to Discern the Burden of Christ!

"Now Jesus called His disciples to Himself and said, "I have compassion on the multitude, because they have now continued with Me three days and have nothing to eat. And I do not want to send them away hungry, lest they faint on the way." Then His disciples said to Him, "Where could we get enough bread in the wilderness to fill such a great multitude?" Jesus said to them, "How many loaves do you have?" And they said, "Seven, and a few little fish." (Matthew 15:32-34)

Discerning the Father's wishes is one thing, but it is an altogether different issue when one learns to listen and patiently wait for the Lord to speak. Many tend to guess the Lord's burden and miss the mark regarding what the Lord needs to do.

I have also observed how some believers move heavily in metaphysical faith and convince themselves that God wants this or that done. I have yet to see any of this foolishness play out in the lives of those who proclaim this idea.

It Begins with God's Burden

Every move of God, I believe, must begin with God's servant receiving revelatory knowledge from Christ. Once a servant of Christ hears the heart of God, then He must patiently wait for the next move.

In our passage above, we find Jesus performing all manner of healing upon those who were sick. Shortly after this, He called the disciples to Himself and talked with them. Notice that He called His disciples, not all the other people.

The Burden

Jesus said, "I have compassion on the multitude because they have now continued with Me three days and have nothing to eat. And I do not want to send them away hungry, lest they faint on the way."

Here's Christ's burden.

I guess the only question now is whether these words will become a move of God or not.

How often have we been at His feet, in prayer and intercession, touching the Father's heart and experiencing the fire of His glory when the Spirit of God suddenly saturates us with His heart? I'm talking about Jesus revealing His burden and impressing it deeply into our hearts! Have you been to this spiritual place?

It Is More Than Just a Conversation?

There are things that God shares with us that don't seem super urgent and may come across as matter-of-factly; however, there are things that He speaks to us that are more than just a conversation. There is such a powerful intent, and the Holy Spirit makes us feel the urgency.

We will make our interpretation practical depending on where we stand spiritually speaking with God. The degree to which we climb in God is the degree to which we will be able to see what He is doing.

Letting Christ Unfold the Burden

"Then His disciples said to Him, "Where could we get enough bread in the wilderness to fill such a great multitude?"

While pondering the words of Jesus and hearing His burden, I started to think, "What would I have done to take this burden and make it practical? This would be my carnal mind kicking into high gear. This is the issue with many of us.

Until I saw this verse, I thought I should run as soon as God speaks. The only thing about this running is that I will likely do things according to my ability and resources. Instead of patiently waiting for Christ's burden to unfold before me, due to my lack of spiritual discipline in perception, I would quickly join in with these disciples and agree with them, **"Where could we get enough bread in the wilderness to fill such a great multitude?"** What a recipe to abort the burden of Christ!

With or Without Us!

I often wonder how often the Lord tolerated my foolishness, lack of faith, fears, doubts, and immature responses. If I were to take a safe guess, it is in the thousands.

After Jesus heard their hearts and how their perception of God's supernatural provision was limited, He took what they could understand. In this case, He asked, **"How many loaves do you have?" And they said, "Seven, and a few little fish."**

We know the story all too well. Jesus stepped in and fed everyone and then some. It shows us that when the Lord has a burden for something, it will get done whether we join Him or not or have the faith to follow Him. With or without us, God will move!

In closing this meditation, I have concluded that the Lord releases His burden first; He then continues to unfold it. We must be disciplined enough to know that this is His intent. If we listen, we can serve the Master in a fresh move of His glory! Neh'enah.

52

Keeping Christ Always at the Center!

"When Jesus came into the region of Caesarea Philippi, He asked His disciples, saying, "Who do men say that I, the Son of Man, am?" So they said, "Some say John the Baptist, some Elijah, and others Jeremiah or one of the prophets. He said to them, "But who do you say that I am?" Simon Peter answered and said, "You are the Christ, the Son of the living God." Jesus answered and said to him, "Blessed are you, Simon Bar-Jonah, for flesh and blood has not revealed this to you, but My Father who is in heaven." (Matthew 16:15, 16)

During this time, miracles and all kinds of signs and wonders had taken place. Many people were so impacted by Christ's healing power that some wanted more of Him. This is one of the reasons that some people followed him for days!

Some who followed were convinced that God's power was flowing through Jesus's hands; however, others stood firm in their own belief and doubted Christ's words and power as coming from God.

If you remember, at this time, John the Baptist had also been put in prison and beheaded, so there was quite a stir among the people of these regions.

During these times, Jesus took His disciples aside and asked them this challenging and heart-stirring question, "Who do men say that I, the Son of Man, am?"

Are You Being Carried Away?

Amid celebrations and victories of what God's power was accomplishing through these servants, it was time for a deep, heart-searching evaluation.

God's evaluations will usually come to us during two significant events.

God will evaluate us when we are having great success, conquering giants, and everything we touch is turning to gold. These are glorious times externally, but God's rule will severely measure them. The condition of our hearts and the posture of how success has left our hearts is all that matters to God. Matters of the heart are the only things that pay celestial dividends. Either we live for Jesus, or we live for self!

The Spirit of the Lord measures the second event severely and will be revealed as we are evaluated in times of duress and character development. Was the last hardship, adversity, or trial the straw that broke the camel's back in your life? Are you bitter, or are you better? Did you throw

Jesus by the wayside because He didn't meet your present needs? Instead of becoming sweeter, you have become hateful and indifferent.

It is easy to be carried away by these two events. Success usually has the power to make us front-slide, while hardships generally have the potential to make us backslide.

The disciples were probably looking at each other and pondering this question when they got the courage to respond to Him, saying, **"Some say John the Baptist, some Elijah, and others Jeremiah or one of the prophets."**

You see, Jesus already knew what people were saying about Him. He wasn't interested in what the crowds were saying. He was interested in what His followers were saying. **Jesus replied, "But who do you say that I am?"** He was only interested in their view of Him!

Jesus wanted to know if He was at the center of their belief system, if they were all in.

For many so-called believers, Christ is just another added idol to their belief system. They bring Jesus on as a lucky charm; please know I'm not trying to sound funny. Believers have many idols: jobs, careers, family, money, ministries, businesses, relationships, material things, etc. So, adding Jesus to this list would only enhance it, not change them internally!

Jesus is Lord of All or Not at All!

As Jesus posed the question and **Simon Peter answered and said, "You are the Christ, the Son of the living God."**

Christianity is not a system that makes life easy for anyone who follows it. It is a set of teachings that unless they are kept and followed through by the one who adheres to them, and I must add, practices them by the power of the Holy Spirit that works mightily in them; it will not only be hard to be a follower of Christ but impossible to be one!

Keeping Christ at the center is the key to walking in joy and peace in the Holy Spirit. If Christ is not the center of your life, not in word only, but in daily practice, you will have the heart to please God.

Evaluate yourself and ponder the following thoughts: Is Christ at the center of my life? Does He rule and govern my life?

Jesus said, "I always do the things that please Him." (John 8:29). Do we have the same mind that was in Christ? Neh'enah.

For the purchase of more books written by David Mayorga, visit our bookstore at:

www.shabarpublications.com

For information regarding ministry, please email David Mayorga at

mayorga1126@gmail.com

Volume 8

Volume 8

Volume 8

The Heart of David Journal

Volume 8

The Heart of David Journal

www.ingramcontent.com/pod-product-compliance
Lightning Source LLC
Chambersburg PA
CBHW020243010526
44107CB00028B/1284